CYCLING THE
KATY TRAIL

CYCLING THE KATY TRAIL

A TANDEM SOJOURN ALONG MISSOURI'S KATY TRAIL

NEIL M. HANSON

WANDERING WHEELIST SERIES

HIGH PRAIRIE PRESS / DENVER

HIGH PRAIRIE PRESS
6403 South Hudson Street, Centennial, CO 80121
www.highprairiepress.com
highprairiepress@gmail.com

Printed in the United States of America
ISBN 978-1-944868-04-8 (Paperback Format)
ISBN 978-1-944868-05-5 (Kindle MOBI Format)
ISBN 978-1-944868-06-2 (ePub Format)

Library of Congress Control Number: 2018943211

Speaking engagements and other author events scheduled through High Prairie Press at highprairiepress@gmail.com or Neil M Hanson at NeilHansonAuthor@gmail.com

For Rick
And the enduring richness of friendship

BOOKS BY NEIL M. HANSON

THE CYCLING REFLECTIONS SERIES
PILGRIM WHEELS (2015)
PILGRIM SPOKES (2016)
CYCLING ACROSS AMERICA: THE PILGRIM SET (2018)

THE WANDERING WHEELIST SERIES
THE PILGRIM WAY (2015)
CYCLING THE KATY TRAIL (2018)
CYCLING THE NATCHEZ TRACE (PLANNED 2019)
CYCLING THE MICKELSON TRAIL (PLANNED 2019)

NON-CYCLING BOOKS
PEACE AT THE EDGE OF UNCERTAINTY (2010)

ADDITIONAL INFORMATION ON NEIL'S BOOKS CAN BE FOUND AT THE BACK OF THIS BOOK.

THE WANDERING WHEELIST
A SERIES OF BOOKS AND ARTICLES

This is one in a series of books that describe specific trails or routes for the touring cyclist. Sometimes (as in this book) they're combined with a journey story that tells the tale of a ride along the trail. They're meant primarily as planning guides to help cyclists plan rides. There are also a number of short articles in the series, a couple of which are listed here.

- *The Pilgrim Way* (Released in 2015 and again in 2016) —A turn-by-turn description of the logistics, route, and details of Neil's journey across America. It's an essential guide for those considering long-distance bicycle touring in general or a cross-country trek specifically. Illustrated.

- *Cycling the Katy Trail* (Released in 2018) — This book you are reading, both a planning guide for a bicycle ride across Missouri on the Katy Trail and a journey story of the ride that Neil and Christine made along the trail in 2016.

- *Cycling the Natchez Trace* (Planned for 2019) — Another hybrid that will be a planning guide for cycling along the Natchez Trace and a journey story of Neil and Dave's continued sojourning, this time joined by Neil's son Ian. From Baton Rouge to Nashville, Neil explores what can only be described as a national treasure for the cyclist.

- ***Cycling the Michelson Trail*** (Planned for 2019) — This will likely be another hybrid, both a trail guide and a journey story, telling the tale of the tandem ride that Neil and Christine made along the trail in 2017 with their good friends Bob and Debbie.

- ***The American Heartland Route*** — When I crossed America on my bicycle, my route incorporated a couple of existing and well-used routes with a few enhancements, providing a collection of roads across the continent that allowed me to experience the back-roads of our nation without heavy traffic, taking me through America's Heartland. This article includes maps and turn by turn directions, as well as road and condition descriptions. (Available at HighPrairiePress.com)

- ***The Ultralight Cyclist*** — A collection of small pieces by me and other cyclists known for their expertise in the art of ultralight cycling. A thorough discussion of the concept of ultralight cycling, including details of gear, weight, etc. (Available at HighPrairiePress.com)

The eastern terminus of the trail at Machens.
Image by Neil Hanson

The Rocheport Tunnel, just east of the town of Rocheport.
Image by Kim Horgan, used with permission

CONTENTS

THE GUIDE

THE JOURNEY

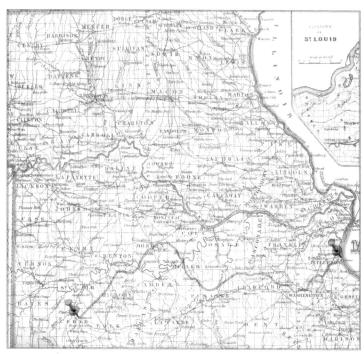

This map image, which also appears on the book cover and in the Trail Overview chapter, comes from an 1856 map by J.H. Colton and Company of New York. The Missouri–Kansas–Texas Railway (which became known as the "KATY" railroad) wasn't in existence at the time this map was created. Note that about two thirds of the way up the left-hand border of the map, the modern-day city of Kansas City doesn't appear, while the town of Westport—today a neighborhood not far from downtown Kansas City—appears prominently. In addition, the cities of Blue Springs, Liberty, and Independence all appear in the map. Today, those towns are swallowed up as suburbs of metropolitan Kansas City. The route drawn here, as well as the route on the cover, is a very rough approximation.
Thanks to Ann Weinstock for discovering this map,
and thanks to the Philadelphia Print Shop for lending it to us.

FOREWORD
BY JIM SAYER

I've been fortunate to serve as the director of Adventure Cycling Association, America's largest cycling membership non-profit, for 14 years. Based on that experience, I can safely declare the following:

There has never been a better time to travel by bicycle in North America. Active and adventure travel are the fastest growing sectors in the global travel industry. In the USA, we have seen hundreds of communities creating new routes, trails and hospitality centers (even cyclist-specific camps and lodging) to attract people like you who are looking for an out-of-the-ordinary travel experience. What has been wonderful for me to witness is the growing appeal of bicycle travel to all demographics, from boomers to millennials; they're all seeking an authentic, down-to-earth and immersive experience on a self-powered vehicle that opens you up to the world.

There have never been more places to ride, including some of the finest rail-trails on the planet. It has been one of the most satisfying parts of my job to enjoy riding many of the best trails and on-road routes anywhere. They have ranged from the Swiss Alps to Taiwanese cities, from the Australian outback to La Route Verte (the "green way") in the province of Quebec. In the USA, they have included the Great Allegheny Passage and C&O Canal (running an amazing car-free 330 miles from Washington, DC to Pittsburgh, PA), the lovely

72-mile Coeur d'Alene Trail traversing the Idaho panhandle, and the Paul Bunyan Trail in central Minnesota, part of an extraordinary rural network of hundreds of seamless rail-trail miles. But among the many stars in the bike travel firmament, the Katy Trail shines out – for its distance of nearly 240 miles, for the beauty of the landscape it traverses, and for the sheer American charm and quirkiness of the communities along the way.

There is no substitute for an enthusiastic and knowledgeable guide. Of course, to experience a treasure like the Katy Trail, it helps to have the expertise of someone who has not only ridden the route multiple times but also knows what to look for. Neil Hanson is just such a person. He's biked along the trail solo and on a tandem, but he's also traveled on other trails in America and elsewhere in the world, so he can offer a richer and more nuanced perspective on the Katy Trail experience.

There is nothing like a 2-for-1 bargain. As Neil notes early on, with a trail guide, you usually get either a nuts-and-bolts book with trip planning details or you get a personal travelogue. With Cycling the Katy Trail, you get both. Neil has thoughtfully provided many of the details you'll need to create your own adventure but also shared with you his personal story, which is often the best motivator to get us off the couch on and on to the bicycle.

There is no time like the present. I have spoken at conferences and gatherings all over the world, to people seeking grand adventures, and if there is one thing I emphasize at least a dozen times, it falls along the line of something that the great athlete Muhammad Ali is reported to have said: "Don't count the days, make the days count." If you are thinking of riding the Katy Trail, don't think too long. Take advantage of this guide and one of the best bike travel experiences in America as quickly as you can! If you haven't experienced it before, you'll discover that bicycle travel is one of the finest and most sensuous ways to experience our world, from the tang of fresh air and the first pedal stroke in the morning to the friendliness of the people you'll meet along the way to the deep satisfaction of dinner and sleep after a day of vigorous pedaling and exploring.

The trail awaits – and so do travel memories that will imprint more deeply than perhaps any you have ever felt or remembered before. Enjoy the ride on one of America's finest and longest rail-trails!

Jim Sayer
Executive Director, Adventure Cycling Association
April, 2018

Autumn along one of the many long straight sections of the trail.
Image by Kim Horgan, used with permission

Thence, we drove a few miles across a swamp, along a raised shell road, with a canal on one hand and a dense wood on the other; and here and there, in the distance, a ragged and angular-limbed and moss-bearded cypress, top standing out, clear cut against the sky, and as quaint of form as the apple-trees in Japanese pictures—such was our course and the surroundings of it.

From *Life on the Mississippi* by **Mark Twain**

Image by Neil Hanson

INTRODUCTION

Mostly just for fun, I had my DNA analyzed not long ago, wondering about the genetic history I was walking around with. Come to find out that Neanderthal genes are mixed somewhat prominently within my chromosomes, at least when compared to the general human population. Christine contends that this explains a lot, though I brush the thought off with a grunt.

That small token of Neanderthal genetic material that exists in most of us is the result of naturally occurring hybridization. It probably helped strengthen us as a species. Many of the species that survive the onslaught of time and evolution probably benefit from some form of hybridization.

I've taken a gamble with this book, and decided to make it a hybrid of sorts. A hybrid that combines the practicality of a trail guide with the romance of a good journey story. As with all hybrids, it takes on a slightly different form than either parent, but I think I've arranged it in a way that works well and makes sense.

In September of 2016, Christine and I rode the Katy Trail across Missouri from one end to the other on our tandem. Our relationship had begun, in a sense, in 2012 when we met at the end of my bicycle journey across America. This journey across the Katy was an experiment in adventure for us, coming less than a year after we married in 2015, and while we learned a lot about the trail, I think we also learned a lot about adventuring together.

Our journey complete, the notion of building a book about the trip wouldn't leave me alone. I was in the midst of assembling a book about a journey I'd taken along the Natchez Trace, but every time I tried to work on the Natchez Trace book, this Katy project would push it aside in my mind. So, I yielded and built this book first.

I wasn't sure what this book was to become; I was just sure that it needed building. There didn't seem to be a need for yet another pure trail guide about the Katy Trail, as there are already a couple of guides that take the reader through great detail of the trail, mile by mile. Maybe a journey story needed to be told about our ride along the trail, but the ride was only a week long, and it didn't feel like there was enough journey story to build a book.

But what about a hybrid? Could I build an effective hybrid, combining the essence of a journey story with the essence of a trail guide? It could be a trail guide that focused on the sort of thing that I would have liked to have seen in a trail guide when I was planning our journey across the Katy, combined with a journey story that shared a bit of the wonder and surprise Christine and I found along the path, not to mention a few of the joys and trials that we experienced on our first real adventure together.

I've built simplicity into the structure of the book, making it easy for the reader who prefers the guide over the journey story or vice versa. If you picked this book up because you're thinking about riding the Katy and only want information to help you plan, you'll want to stick with "The Katy Trail Guide" section, which comes first in the book. It doesn't dig into comprehensive detail about what you'll find at each and every mile marker along the way, because I found other books out there that already do that. Nor does it simply replicate the information available at the Bike Katy Trail website. Instead, I present information from a very practical perspective, through the eyes of a touring cyclist planning a route and wanting to know where lodging and supplies can be found. I give the reader the actual experience, because I rode the trail twice, once in 2012 and again in 2016.

On the other hand, if you've picked up this book because you enjoy a good journey story and have only slight interest in riding the trail (or none at all), then you can skip right past "The Katy Trail Guide" and jump headlong into the "The Katy Trail Journey." This is where I tell the story of the bicycle adventure that Christine and I shared as we pedaled along this gorgeous jewel of the American system of rail trails. It's where I share the story of the towns we rode through, the people we met, the places we stayed, and the truths I discovered about me and about us.

Either way, thanks for your support, and thanks for reading! I hope you enjoy my little experiment in hybridization.

One of several benches nicely placed along the trail, offering
an excellent spot to eat a granola bar and drink a little water.
Image by Neil Hanson

The section east of Boonville is considered by many to be the most beautiful section of the entire trail, owing largely to the dramatic effect of the towering ancient bluffs. Image by Kim Horgan, used by permission

THE
KATY TRAIL
GUIDE

The beautiful dappling on the trail created by the sun bleeding through the canopy above is a source of constant wonder for the cyclist. The trail winds its way through a broken hardwood canopy for much of it's path along the Missouri River from Boonville to the eastern terminus at Machens. Image by Neil Hanson

GUIDE TO THE GUIDE

The practical perspective from which I've written this guide should provide an easy-to-use snapshot of where dining, supplies, and lodging were available along the trail as of the time of the ride, September 2016. This is not an exhaustive description of everything a cyclist will see or encounter, but rather the sort of information I would have liked to have had when I was planning our ride.

When I organize a bicycle tour, I've learned that I enjoy the tour most when I can arrange my lodging ahead of time for each night. So long as I know that I have a destination for the day, and that the destination includes a warm shower and soft bed, then my point *A* and my point *B* are defined, and I can take the day as it comes. But I do need to know (with a high degree of certainty) whether or not I'll be able to find supplies, and at what interval. When I bicycled across a remote section of the Mojave Desert a few years ago, I could see that there was a 90-mile stretch of desert with no supplies, and I planned accordingly. That was a fluke, and most days of riding only require the knowledge that at some reasonable intervals I'll be able to find supplies, and if those intervals are long, I need to know ahead of time to carry a little extra water.

I don't want to make a cheat sheet for the day, with details of every stop where I'll find supplies. I want to be able to start pedaling in the morning, and take the day as it comes. If there are particularly wonderful sights along the way that I might miss, I do want to know about those, so I watch for them, but generally I don't want to overplan.

On the Katy Trail, there are milestones every 15 miles or so. Back in the early days of railroads, these milestones were required for the steam engine to take on water, so it was a natural course of events that small towns developed at those spots. However, between those early days and now, these stopping points have evolved, or in many cases disappeared altogether, and may *or may not* provide the rider with supplies of any sort. Sometimes you may need to ride a mile or two down a road to find supplies.

For folks like me who don't want an excruciating level of detail in their plan, the available trail information didn't give me what I needed. It's for folks like me that I've written this guide, folks who want to know their daily starting point and ending point, and only need to know where reliable supplies are in between those two points so they can plan *just enough* to be able to take the day and the ride as it comes.

I've set this guide up based on my experiences on the trail, first in 2012 for a portion of it, then in 2016 from Clinton to Saint Charles. I start off with a table that describes *only* the milestones where there's a fairly good chance that the rider can find supplies, so that you (the reader) aren't forced to weed through the many milestones (or towns) along the way where you *aren't* likely to find supplies. You're going to see those milestones anyway while you're riding, but there's no need to clog up my planning section with milestone details that aren't important. As I plan, I want to know where I'm likely to find supplies. That's really what I care most about.

The table gives you a quick overview of the route and supplies available, as of 2016. The parts after the table give a bit more detail about the nature of the trail itself in each section, and, when necessary, a hint or two about supplies or lodging.

Regarding mile markers and distances, I've chosen to use the mile markers as listed by official Katy Trail sources. I'm not crazy about this system for a few reasons, but I include it so that I'm consistent with other sources. My reticence about the conventional mile-marker system is based on the following:

1. Mile markers themselves are not consistently posted along the trail, or at least they didn't appear to be when I rode it.

2. The mile-marker system has a mythical beginning point that doesn't really exist along the trail today, which becomes confusing. For example, the far eastern terminus of the trail is at mile marker 26.9. There's nothing prior to this mile marker, yet it's the "beginning." The reasons for this don't matter, but it creates confusion.

3. If you're riding west to east (as I did on both occasions), the mile markers are reversed from the order you'd like to see for planning purposes.

For these reasons, I've added my own mile-marker convention in addition to the official mile marker to help the reader in planning, beginning at mile zero in Clinton. I refer to the mile markers as follows:

• The official mile marker starts in Machens at MM-26.9 and continues west to the end of the trail in Clinton at MM-264.6.

• My convention starts in Clinton at EZ-0 and continues east to the end of the trail at Machens at EZ-238.

• I include both conventions in my table for folks who want to stick with the posted convention, though in my dialogue I'll refer only to my EZ mile markers, as they coincide with the ride as I took it.

• In my EZ convention I round miles off, since I don't generally require a high level of precision in my planning.

Next, after my table of milestones, I include a chapter on the trail overall, my impressions, and my summary comments. For the casual reader looking only for a planning tool and a high-level synopsis of the Katy Trail, the table and the overview should give you enough information to decide if this is a trip you want to take.

Following the overview, I go into greater depth with a series of more detailed descriptions of the trail, divided into parts that correspond to my impressions of the nature of the trail:

- **Part One** - Rolling farmland from Clinton to Boonville.

- **Part Two** - The mostly wooded trail tucked beneath limestone cliffs from Boonville to Bluffton.

- **Part Three** - The flat farmland along the floodplain from Bluffton to Defiance.

- **Part Four** - The more populated and popular section from Defiance to Saint Charles.

- **Part Five** - The barely used section from Saint Charles to Machens.

Enjoy the guide, and happy cycling!

Image by Kim Horgan, used with permission

MILESTONES

Milestone	Neil's EZ Mile Mrkr (EZ)	Orig Katy Mile Mrkr (MM)	Gap	Comments ("Right" and "left" assume you are riding from west to east on the trail.)
Clinton	0	264.6	n/a	Note that the town was a couple of miles up the road from the trailhead. Clinton was included here only because it was the beginning point, not because there were supplies along the trail.
Calhoun	9	255.5	9	The town (and supplies) were generally to the right of the trail.
Windsor	17	248.0	8	There was a Casey's just off the trail to the left, and quite a bit more "town" to the right.
Green Ridge	25	239.2	9	There was a Casey's to the left of the trail.
Sedalia	36	229.0	10	Town was to the left of the trail for the most part. Consider riding north (left) on either Grand or Ohio if you want to sit down and eat. There was a convenience store to the right as the trail crossed Ohio if all you needed was supplies.
Pilot Grove	61	203.3	26	The town was to the right of the trail.
Boonville	73	191.8	12	Many dining, lodging, and supply options were available.

Milestone	Neil's EZ Mile Mrkr (EZ)	Orig Katy Mile Mrkr (MM)	Gap	Comments ("Right" and "left" assume you are riding from west to east on the trail.)
New Franklin	77	188.0	4	It was a quarter mile to the left of the trail, but I included it here as "on the trail" because the supplies seemed fairly reliable.
Rocheport	86	178.3	10	Soon after crossing the bridge into town, we went left on Central Street for a block to get to the general store. There may be many other options in town too, depending on the day you go, but on a Monday in September 2016 at 10:00 in the morning we weren't able to find coffee.
Cooper's Landing (Columbia)	101	164.0	14	This was a campground and marina along the trail, and it seemed to be one of the most reliable supply stops along this section.
Hartsburg	111	153.6	10	Supplies were available on certain days only; nothing was open Monday or Tuesday in September 2016.
Jefferson City	121	143.2	10	We had to take the spur to the right at N. Jefferson to reach supplies. Because you would have needed to leave the trail, I wouldn't have included this stop, but it was 14 miles in one direction and 18 in the other to reliable supplies, so this was a good place to resupply.
Mokane	140	125.0	18	About 500' to the left of the trail we found a small general store with supplies.
Rhineland	160	105.0	20	We rode the road between the two trail crossings to find supplies—it was only a quarter mile or so between the first road crossing and the second.

Milestone	Neil's EZ Mile Mrkr (EZ)	Orig Katy Mile Mrkr (MM)	Gap	Comments ("Right" and "left" assume you are riding from west to east on the trail.)
Marthasville	187	77.7	27	The town was on the left, and in 2016 there was a great restaurant called Philly's where you could fill water bottles and get food. There was also a grocery 1000' to the left up Rt 47 (which the trail crossed under).
Augusta	198	66.4	11	In Augusta we found many dining options plus grocery options. The town was all to the left of the trail.
Defiance	206	59.1	7	There were a couple of dining options and a bike store where you could at least fill water bottles.
Saint Charles	225	39.5	20	Supplies, bike shops, and dining options were available.
Machens	238	26.9	13	Included here *only* because it was the eastern end of the trail. There was nothing here but a small trailhead parking lot, and there were no supplies anywhere nearby.

Autumn might be the most beautiful time of year to experience the Katy Trail.
Image by Kim Horgan, used with permission

TRAIL OVERVIEW

The Katy Trail is believed by many people to be the crown jewel of the American rail-trail system. After having ridden the entire trail—some parts of it twice—my opinion is that it's a wonderful trail that is fairly well maintained and should absolutely be on any rider's "bucket list." I don't have enough experience or context to agree or disagree that it's *the* crown jewel, but here are my impressions of the trail overall, as of September 2016.

- The scenery was absolutely gorgeous. We got 75 miles of rolling farmland at the western end, then the rest of the trail tucked back and forth between floodplain farmland and wooded riverside trail, often beneath towering limestone cliffs.

- It was one of the longest contiguous trails in the country at 200-plus miles, which made it a perfect candidate for a multiday trip.

- My 2012 experience and every conversation I've had about it since then has led me to believe the trail was generally maintained extremely well; our experience with rutted trail in 2016 was likely an anomaly.

- Much of the trail crossed wonderfully remote and rural terrain. The upside to this was that the Katy Trail was an excellent ride for experiencing a bit of seclusion from hustle and bustle. The downside was that planning was important, since there were many stretches with less in the way of supplies than we might have expected.

- The above bullet is especially important if you plan to ride on weekdays. In particular, riding on Monday and Tuesday meant for us that a good portion of the services along the trail were not available, so future riders may need to plan accordingly.

- As of the writing of this book in late 2016, there were some outstanding efforts underway to build additional pieces of trail that will connect with the Katy Trail and will provide trailhead access at bigger population centers (specifically Kansas City).

- Wonderful music can be an integral part of the Katy Trail experience. It was a key component of the joy I found along the trail in 2012, although on our 2016 ride we didn't encounter it to the same degree.

- Depending on when you go, there can be a significant social aspect to the trail. Weekends tend to be more social, as there are more riders sharing this treasure and more places are open for socializing.

- The communities along the route have embraced the notion of the trail to differing and inconsistent degrees. As I rode the trail, I usually felt very welcomed by the people I met in the small communities along the way. However, I occasionally felt like local folks and merchants didn't like cyclists and didn't like the fact that we were invading their small towns. This was my perception, and I wonder if this might be a natural phenomenon that occurs when a trail brings new outsiders into a tight-knit rural community, and in fact I explore this thought in the "Journey" section of this book.

- In my travels along the trail I stayed at motels or bed-and-breakfast accommodations. When planning, I found that the information about available lodging along the trail was not always accurate. (This included available guide-books and the Ride Katy Trail website.) My advice for cyclists planning a trip is to use a tool like Google Maps to search for lodging along the trail. For cyclists planning to camp along the way, I will assume that sources like the Ride Katy Trail website are accurate regarding camping facilities, but I can't vouch for that. My general impression has been that there are good and adequate camping opportunities along the trail, and I talked with a number of cyclists on both of my trips who were camping and happy with availability of facilities.

All in all, the Katy is a wonderful trail through a beautiful part of the nation. I'd eagerly ride all or part of the trail again in the future. While I don't believe I'm qualified to proclaim that the Katy Trail is *the* crown jewel of the American rail-trail system, there's no doubt in my mind that at the very least it deserves a prominent place in the jewelry box where the crown jewels are kept!

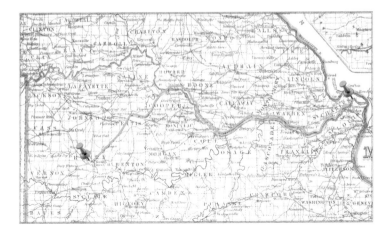

The rolling farmland along the western fifty to seventy miles of the trail often feature a course of deciduous trees that runs through fields alternating between crops and pasture.
Image by Neil Hanson

There are several dramatic cuts through low hills between Sedalia and Boonville.
Image by Neil Hanson

THE WESTERN SECTION

ROLLING FARMLAND FROM CLINTON TO BOONVILLE

ABOUT 73 MILES

This western section of the trail rolled through rural western Missouri, a heavily agricultural region. There were road crossings at fairly regular intervals where cyclists could stop to get water or food. This section was a little over 70 miles long, with ample lodging at either end. If you wanted to make it a two-day trip, Sedalia offered lots of lodging options and was at about the halfway mark.

Christine and I began our trip with an overnight stay in Clinton at the Haysler House Bed and Breakfast Inn. We ate supper at the Courtyard Grill & Bar the night before we started our ride. Clinton was a great little town for spending the night, and we enjoyed our stay at the Haysler House as well as our wandering around through the old town of Clinton.

A negative here is that somehow the trailhead was actually outside of town by a couple of miles. As a result, we had to park our vehicle at the trailhead a few miles from town, which meant staying or dining in Clinton wasn't necessarily ideal, since we were going to be driving to the trailhead anyway. Roger at the Haysler House was kind enough to let us leave our truck parked at his place, which was why we chose to stay in Clinton proper.

Below are the towns we crossed, starting in Clinton, and

what we found. The mileage indicated was the distance from Clinton, our starting point. Note that my description is from the perspective of someone traveling from Clinton to Machens and therefore eastbound. I use "right" and "left" rather than compass directions, since the actual compass direction of the trail changed a bit as it meandered. As a reminder, the following is based on conditions as they were in September 2016.

- Calhoun — About 10 miles — The town was mostly to the right of the trail. The easiest thing to do would be to get off the trail at Depot Street when arriving at the south end of town, and then turn left on Main Street to make your way through town. Both High Street and College Street accessed the trail again.

- Windsor — About 17 miles — The town was mostly to the right of the trail, and it appeared that there was quite a bit there, both in the way of dining and groceries.

- Green Ridge — About 25 miles — A smaller town without many options. We stopped here and bought coffee at the Casey's General Store that was to the left of the trail. There was a park next door, so we sat at the park and enjoyed our coffee and a granola bar.

- Sedalia — About 35 miles — Sedalia was a large town (by Katy Trail standards) with all the services available that you'd likely need. The problem was that the trail itself didn't go past any of the places you'd want to stop for food or services. We ended up adding several miles to our day backtracking through town. If I had it to do again, I'd ride the trail into town, and at South Ohio Avenue I'd have turned left (heading north) which would have taken us right into town, where we could have found lots of service options. This route would have also kept us generally following the direction of the trail. A bonus of this route is that it would have taken us right past Pro-Velo Cycle Sport bike shop, where Ebby could fix you up with about anything you needed for your bike. On my cross-country trip, Ebby saved my bacon by repairing busted spokes on my rear wheel. Ohio Avenue would have taken us through downtown Sedalia, and we'd have needed to either cross the railroad tracks on Ohio Avenue or go three blocks east to Washington where there was a bridge over the railroad tracks.

Once we were north of the tracks, we made our way east to find the Katy Trail again. We could have turned right on Pettis, which became Saline, and then left on Emmet. We could probably have turned left about anywhere before Emmet too, but Emmet was actually marked as the trail. After we turned left we went a couple of blocks to Boonville Street, where we turned right. Boonville crossed the Katy Trail again a quarter mile or so east of Emmet.

Be aware that in Sedalia, the Katy Trail had a gap, so no matter what, we were going to end up riding on streets in Sedalia to get across the gap. If you stayed on the trail, you could follow the markers to get through the gap and back to the actual trail, but since the trail didn't take you past any of the services you would probably want, my recommendation is to plan your own streets through town, as suggested above.

• Pilot Grove — About 61 miles — Note that Pilot Grove was over 35 miles past Sedalia, and it was really the first place to get water or food after we left Sedalia. When Christine and I did this, I didn't plan for this long dry stretch, and we were plenty thirsty by the time we hit Pilot Grove. Clifton City was about halfway between Sedalia and Pilot Grove, but there didn't appear to be any services. At Pilot Grove, the town was to the right of the trail. We found a Casey's where we could fill water bottles and get a little food, and it appeared that there might be a café in town too, though we couldn't tell whether or not it was open.

• Boonville — About 73 miles — These final 12 miles from Pilot Grove to Boonville included a wonderful gentle descent for the last few miles. There was a bike shop right on the trail where the trail dropped off in the town of Boonville.

Boonville was our destination for our first day of riding. We stayed at the High Street Victorian Bed & Breakfast and ate supper at the Palace restaurant, both right downtown. There appeared to be quite a few lodging and dining options, though I'd highly recommend both the High Street Victorian and the Palace. Boonville is an old river town that has become a bit of a regional "destination" in recent years as a result of a casino in town.

Our September ride featured a beautiful morning as we began riding east from Clinton, fog rolling beautifully across the trail between fields on either side.
Image by Neil Hanson

THE RIVER BLUFFS

BENEATH TOWERING LIMESTONE CLIFFS FROM BOONVILLE TO BLUFFTON

ABOUT 81 MILES

I've heard many people express that this section is the most scenic of the entire trail, and after riding it, it was easy to understand why. It was about 81 miles from Boonville to Bluffton, and this part of the Katy contained a high concentration of woodland trail, often running below towering limestone cliffs or meandering through deep hardwood forest.

Christine and I started our second day of riding in Boonville, crossing the Missouri River on the excellent walking/biking path that was nicely separated from the highway. Just north of the river, the signs indicated that the Katy Trail leaves the highway, so we followed those signs. This took us on a combination of streets and the trail, passing the old roundhouse in Franklin. It's worth noting that if we'd just stayed on Highway 5 for a few miles after crossing the river, we'd have come to the Katy Trail that way, avoiding a little bit of jockeying. This might have been more efficient, but we'd have also missed the chance to see the site of the old roundhouse along the trail.

The first several miles of the trail skirted alternatively forest and field on one side or another, generally following the path of Salt Creek. After the slight up-and-down roll of the trail west of Boonville, the absolutely horizontal nature of the trail east of Boonville offered encouragement to lean into the pedals and work hard along the perpetual flats.

At about 13 miles, we rolled through a beautiful old tunnel and across a bridge into the quintessential river town of Rocheport. It felt to us as though the town had worked hard to cater to riders along the trail, but we were there on a Monday morning, and nothing was open. We'd hoped to stop for a coffee but couldn't find an open coffee shop, though as of the writing of this book I understand a coffee shop has opened along the trail. This was the beginning of many disappointments at the lack of available services early in the week in towns the trail passed through.

After leaving Rocheport, the guidance we got online and from books indicated that there were several small towns along the trail, so we weren't too worried about finding some coffee somewhere, maybe even a little snack and a top-off for our water bottles. However, the only place we found to pick up any supplies between Boonville and Jefferson City was a marina/campground called Cooper's Landing, which was about six miles past (or east of) McBaine. Cooper's Landing was a welcome sight as the trail emerged from the woods to skirt the river. The place had been open for decades, though BikeKatyTrail.com didn't even show this as a milestone along the trail; it was the *only* place we found to pick up supplies in the 50 miles between Boonville and Jefferson City on the Monday when we rode that section.

In Hartsburg, the trail ran through town like it did back in Rocheport, but like Rocheport, there was absolutely nothing open on a Monday. We stopped at the Globe Hotel to drop off a copy of one of my previous books, in which I talk about staying there at the Globe, and the ice water that Mark and Leaia filled our water bottles with was welcome and appreciated.

When Christine and I rode the trail in September 2016, the

trail east of Hartsburg was completely flooded, with no signage as to how to get around the flooding. We opted to get off the trail and follow roads into Jefferson City. This resulted in quite a few extra miles and some serious hill climbing at the end of the day. In addition, it meant we spent several miles on US 63, which was extremely crowded with drivers who didn't seem happy to have a bicycle on "their" road.

Our second day of riding ended in Jefferson City, after crossing the Missouri River on a wonderful walking/biking path that was separated from traffic. We stayed at the Cliff Manor Inn, which was just across the river, and absolutely loved the place. Nothing near us was open for supper, so we ordered pizza delivery. On other evenings it's possible more places would have been open, but Monday night seemed to be a time when many restaurants were closed.

The next morning we rode back across the river and continued east on the trail, picking it up at the North Jefferson trailhead, which was at about EZ-121. After 12 miles we rolled through the little town of Tebbetts, but no supplies were available there. Six miles further we crossed the highway and could see the little town of Mokane only a few hundred yards to our left, and though it didn't look too promising, we rode up there because we were 20 miles into our day and really hoped to find some water.

As it turned out, there was a small general store in Mokane, though the proprietor didn't seem cordially inclined toward cyclists. Still, we were able to purchase ice and drinks and make our way down the trail. I should mention that on Google Maps recently, this building was labeled as a bar and grill, so it may have changed hands.

We passed both Steedman and Portland, with no indication that there were services available in either place. In guidebooks and at the Bike Katy Trail website, Bluffton was listed as a town along the way. It was about 81 miles from Boonville. However, when we crossed the road where Bluffton was supposed to be, there was no indication that any services were available. There wasn't even the hint of a town. There was a house off to the left, which I believe may have been a bed and breakfast at one time, but beyond that there was no hint that a town existed.

It wasn't all that unusual for places that were listed by the Bike Katy Trail website as "towns" to sometimes only be a place where the trail crossed the highway. This section of the trail was extremely rural, which was wonderful and beautiful and we loved it, but it also meant that services were sparse.

Approaching the Rocheport tunnel into the morning sun.
Image by Kim Horgan, used with permission

WOODLANDS AND FIELDS

PASTORAL FLOODPLAIN FARMLAND FROM BLUFFTON TO DEFIANCE

ABOUT 52 MILES

There was nothing of note in Bluffton that would have me end Part Two there. In fact, as I said in Part Two, there was nothing in Bluffton, or even such a thing as Bluffton, beyond the fact that the trail crossed a road there. But it seemed like a good place to transition from one part to the next, because the nature of the trail transitioned just a bit at that point.

In the 52 miles from Bluffton at MM-110.9 to Defiance at MM-59.1, there were only a few places where the trail ran beside the river. For the most part, the trail stayed in the floodplain and remained perfectly flat. It occasionally ducked in and out of forested sections, alternating with farmland, often hedging right along the border between forested hill on one side and flat farmland on the other.

From Bluffton to Rhineland was about six miles, and supplies were available in Rhineland when I rode through there in 2012 and again in 2016. In addition to supplies, there were lodging options available.

The trail crossed the highway twice in Rhineland, once on the west side of town and once on the east side of town. To get supplies, it was easiest to get off the trail and ride the highway for the half mile between the two crossings. The actual town of Rhineland has been up on a hill since the US government helped them move their town off the floodplain following the 1993 flood, but both times I rode that section there was still a presence along the highway where supplies were available.

Another five miles east of Rhineland was McKittrick. When Christine and I rode the trail, we got off the trail at McKittrick and rode south along Highway 19 for a couple of miles into the town of Hermann, where we took a day off to enjoy the area. Highway 19 intersected with Highway 94 about a quarter mile south of the trail, and there was a big BP gas station at that intersection where you could find supplies.

As an aside, Hermann was a wonderful little town, and Christine and I were really glad that we decided to take a rest day there. We stayed at the Carriage House Bed and Breakfast (also known as the Cady Winterset Cottage,) which was run by a delightful woman whose name was also Christine. The meals we had at the Cady, and the place itself, were the highlight of our stay. Like with most towns along the trail, expect to find many establishments closed on Monday and Tuesday. If you do opt to stay in McKittrick instead of Hermann, I understand that the establishments there have been happy to drive cyclists over to Hermann to explore. My friend Rick stayed at Joey's Bird House Bed and Breakfast in McKittrick and loved it.

From McKittrick to Marthasville was about 22 miles, and we found no supplies or services in between. In Marthasville, however, we found an excellent lunch place called Philly's Pizza. Denis ran the place, and not only did they make outstanding pizza, they also had a fairly complete menu of non-pizza items. A terrific bonus was that they really catered to cyclists and welcomed those of us on two wheels with open arms. About 1000 feet away was a general store, a good source for additional supplies.

From Marthasville to Augusta was 11 miles, and in Augusta

there were plenty of services available. Christine and I stayed the night at the Red Brick Inn of Augusta Bed & Breakfast and loved the place. We had heard great things from other cyclists about the Silly Goose restaurant, but we ended up eating at Ashley's Rose Restaurant instead.

The final seven miles of this section of the Katy continued with more floodplain farmland. In Defiance there were a few dining options, but I couldn't find a grocery or convenience store. There was a bike shop in town, though, and I assume a cyclist could have found supplies there.

For a tandem, the wide bridges offer a sturdy place to lean the bike and enjoy a break.
Image by Neil Hanson

Image by Neil Hanson

THE EASTERN SECTION

THE EDGES OF SUBURBIA FROM DEFIANCE TO SAINT CHARLES

ABOUT 20 MILES

Soon after Defiance, the trail began to feel like it was moving through different flavors of suburbia or the edges of suburbia. This section was only 20 miles long, and it had every appearance of being heavily used. When I chatted with cyclists in Saint Charles in 2012, it seemed that a common day trip was to start in Saint Charles, ride the 20 miles out to Defiance or maybe the 27 miles to Augusta, have lunch, then ride back to Saint Charles.

There were a couple of places along this section where I felt like it could be a slightly sketchy part of town, and while I might have been wrong about this, I would probably not have wanted to be finishing a ride through these areas after dusk.

Saint Charles was a fantastic cycling destination. There were multiple dining options, several supply options, and even more than one bike shop option. I stopped at a place called the Bike Stop Café and Outpost in 2012 and again in 2016 in their new digs. As the name suggests, it was a little café inside a bike shop, or maybe a bike shop inside a café. In 2016 we stopped there after a day of riding in rain and dried our soaked bodies while enjoying hot coffee.

If I had our 2016 ride to plan again, I'd end the day in Saint Charles and enjoy a day of exploring another old river town.

Image by Neil Hanson

THE FORGOTTEN THIRTEEN MILES

SAINT CHARLES TO MACHENS

ABOUT 13 MILES

Riders could easily be forgiven for believing that Saint Charles was the eastern end of the trail. For all practical purposes, I suppose it was. There were no services along the final 13 miles of the trail. It crossed a few country roads, but I remember thinking that it would be difficult to find even a water spigot to fill a water bottle if a person needed to.

In 2012 I rode the trail all the way to Machens, because the trail was part of my cross-country ride. In Machens I made my way up to Highway 94 and used that road to continue my ride over to Alton and beyond. I remember that during the planning stages for that trip, the map suggested that the trailhead was right by a road that I could have taken for the half mile up to Highway 94. In reality, the trail dumped me off into a bed of fist-sized-and-larger stone ballast along the still-existing railway, and I walked my bike across this ballast and over the tracks to the gravel road on the other side.

I have heard there may be plans to extend the Katy further east, as it appeared that the old railbed went right past West Alton on its way to downtown Saint Louis. If that's the case, then at some future point a West Alton trailhead would be an ideal place for cross-country cyclists to access the trail.

Our plan in 2016 was to ride to the end of the trail, make our way on back roads up to a ferry to cross the Mississippi River over to Grafton, Illinois, then ride the Mississippi River Trail down to Alton. While we were prevented from completing this final piece of our planned ride by flooding and washed-out trail, I think this would have made for a really enjoyable eastern end of a ride.

I will say that if I lived in the Saint Louis area and was looking for a nice 26-mile trail ride, starting at Machens, riding to Saint Charles for coffee, then riding back to Machens would be a pretty darned good option. It was flat, very rural, and beautiful. In 2012 the trail was impeccably maintained and provided smooth riding.

Image by Neil M. Hanson

THE TRAIL AS WE RODE IT

Below is a table showing the journey along the trail as Christine and I rode it in 2016. Note that these mileages are not necessarily the same as the trail mileages, since we had a couple of days where trail conditions forced us off the trail and onto roads, or where we backtracked for one reason or another.

One of the things that the table helps point out is that day after day, our average rolling speed was about 12 mph along the trail, regardless of whatever else was going on. Our first day the trail undulated up and down, and we averaged about 12 mph. The second day we ended up on highways that were steep ups and downs for the final dozen or so miles of the day, and we averaged about 12 mph for that day. Our final day was spent riding on a soaked trail through torrential rain, which I was sure slowed us significantly, yet our average speed was about 12 mph. The point is that the trail provided the rider with riding conditions that allowed for a very consistent average pace.

The table also points out just how flat the trail was along the Missouri River. On our third day of riding we rode about 50 miles and had a total elevation gain of 361 feet. To be clear, we were actually going down-river, so we had a net elevation loss for the day, meaning our ending elevation was slightly lower than our beginning elevation. However, as we rode, we'd occasionally have a little bump up to a bridge then a bump back down. This resulted in the fact that even though our net elevation gain was less than zero, we did, in fact, climb a little bump now and then. Those bumps totaled up to a gross "climb" of 361 feet. This means that on that third day of riding, in every mile, we averaged a total of only about 7 feet of climbing. That's flat. Really flat. If you average the entire ride from Clinton to St Charles, including the steep hills that were part of our detour on the second day and the undulating first section of the trail, each mile we rode included an average of only about 15 feet of climbing.

Finally, for someone who's looking for a five-day-ride plan across the Katy, this table represents one that worked well for us in 2016. Days one and two would actually have had fewer miles than listed in the table without the detours and backtracking that we did. Day five would have been longer, had we ridden past Saint Charles to either Machens or beyond.

Day	Begin	End	Daily Miles	Cum. Miles	Gross Climb (ft)	Avg Rolling Speed (mph)	Date
1	Clinton	Boonville	79.7	79.7	1614	12.4	9/11
2	Boonville	Jefferson City	66.8	146.5	1102	12.8	9/12
3	Jefferson City	Hermann	47.6	194.1	361	12.7	9/13
4	Hermann	Augusta	37.8	231.9	443	11.3	9/15
5	Augusta	Saint Charles	28.1	260	579	11.9	9/16
		TOTAL	260		4099		
		Daily Average	52				

THE
KATY TRAIL
JOURNEY

PROLOGUE

*I have found out there ain't no surer way to find out whether you like
people or hate them than to travel with them.*

~ **Mark Twain**, *Tom Sawyer Abroad*

Guiding Christine's car along I-70 through central Missouri, slicing through air heavy with humidity and sticky with
heat, the light traffic allowed my mind to drift into daydreams.
Christine sat beside me, her dog Tramp in the back seat, the
rear section of her Ford Edge filled with those things she didn't
want the movers to pack up into the moving van.

We were en route from Virginia, where Christine had lived
for the past dozen or so years, to Colorado, where I lived and
where she would make her new home. We were taking a leap
and moving in together, the next step in a relationship that we'd
been exploring for a little under a year. It wasn't something we'd
undertaken lightly, and our blended mood in the car reflected
this. On the one hand was our mutual excitement over the beginning of this new chapter in life for both of us, and on the
other hand was some emotion that might boil down to a phrase
like, "What on earth are we doing?"

We were well into day two of the trip (or was it day three?),
Christine gazing out her window at the hills of Missouri as we
rolled through them. "Didn't you cross Missouri somewhere
close to here last year when you rode your bike out to the east

coast?" she asked.

"Pretty close. For some of the miles across the state I rode on the Katy Trail, which runs along the river. We'll be passing over the trail in a few miles and you can look down and see it." She was quiet as she contemplated this, continuing to watch the hills passing by. After half a minute or so, I continued. "I think Rocheport is close to the highway up ahead a bit, and the trail crosses through town. How 'bout we get off there to get some coffee and take a look at the trail?"

Ten minutes later we'd found a shady spot to park the car in Rocheport. We picked up some coffee at a coffee shop by the trail and took Tramp out for a walk along the trail where it passed through town.

Christine's a walker. A serious walker. She'll clip along at a pace that many folks would consider jogging, something like a 14-minute mile. Those of us who are mere mortals in the walking world need to learn to keep up. This isn't a problem for Tramp, whose disreputable lineage appears to be some unique fusion of greyhound and terrier.

I say this only to point out that a walk with Christine can never be described as a "stroll." Words that might describe a walk with Christine would be more like "scamper" or "scurry," "scoot," maybe, or "scramble." We were, by any description, hastening down the trail, coffee in hand, Tramp happily prancing beside us.

We took a turn down a side trail that headed out toward the river, which eventually brought us to a broad overlook constructed of planking. It was the perfect place to stop and admire the scenery, away from people. Truth be told, I welcomed the chance to catch my breath, while Tramp seemed to welcome the opportunity to caress the hot breeze with his nose, tasting the rich smells of the floodplain below us and the wide Missouri River beyond.

I leaned my elbows on the railing, and Christine stepped up beside me, leaning against me just a bit. We were quiet for a few minutes, rich steamy air swirling gently around us, causing her to brush her hair out of her face occasionally.

"So you rode right through here?" Christine asked.

"I think this is a part of the trail I missed. I broke some spokes riding along the trail, and this is a bit of the trail that I missed as a result. I'd love to come back and ride the whole trail someday."

She smiled, quiet in thought, swatting a mosquito now and then as she looked into the distance. Then she pulled away suddenly, and cast a look of surprise at me. "Hey, why is it that bugs don't ever bite you? Here I am exterminating mosquitos by the dozen, and you don't even seem to notice them."

"Yeah, they'll bite me now and then, but generally they leave me alone."

"Hmmff." She shook her head and leaned back against me, her skin warm and soft against my arm. With her other arm she continued the swatting routine, obviously not happy about it. I reached down and slapped my leg, hoping that this pretended sharing of discomfort would make her feel better.

"You only did that to make me feel better, didn't you?"

I was quiet for a moment, a little uncomfortable with the level of transparency already developing between us. "Maybe. Did it work?"

She smiled and leaned her head against me. "Would you ride it alone?"

"Ride what alone?"

"The trail. If you rode it again, I mean?"

"I suppose I could. Do you think you'd like riding on it? It'd be fun to ride it together."

She smiled at that. "I'm not sure I'm up for riding clear

across the state on a bicycle. Remember I haven't been riding a bike my whole life like you have."

"Heck, you just climb in the saddle and pedal. You're in better shape than most people half our age—I barely keep up with you when we walk. It'd be a piece of cake for you."

She shook her head slightly, a doubtful half smile playing across her mouth, not convinced, but intrigued by the idea. "Is the whole trail flat like this?"

"Yep. It's an old railbed with easy grades up and down when it's not completely flat."

The air had changed slightly, pushing a lighter scent down on us from above, replacing the pungent river-bottom smell that Tramp had been enjoying. Christine looked over at me, seemingly reading my expression, and smiled. "That might be fun." Turning back toward the river, nodding slightly, she continued, "I think I could do this."

CHAPTER ONE
DRIVING - SEPTEMBER, 2016

To particularize: the average American's simplest and commonest form of breakfast consists of coffee and beefsteak; well, in Europe, coffee is an unknown beverage. You can get what the European hotel-keeper thinks is coffee, but it resembles the real thing as hypocrisy resembles holiness. It is a feeble, characterless, uninspiring sort of stuff, and almost as undrinkable as if it had been made in an American hotel. The milk used for it is what the French call "Christian" milk—milk which has been baptized.

~**Mark Twain**, *A Tramp Abroad*

A glorious late-summer day illuminates the prairie around us as we drive east across Kansas. Christine, recently become my bride, sits beside me, our new tandem bicycle securely strapped into the bed of the pickup. We'll end up in Parkville, Missouri, at the end of the day, where we'll enjoy supper with my brother and his wife, spend the night in a bed and breakfast, then head to Clinton, Missouri, tomorrow to start our trek across Missouri on the Katy Trail.

I love the excitement that consumes me when a new adventure begins to unfold. The planning is all done, the route laid out well enough, the reservations are made. Now, subtle thrill underlies each heartbeat, and pleasant trepidation infuses each mile that passes, as I make my way to the point of commencement. Today, Christine and I embark on our first cycling adventure together, and our smiles and conversation make it clear to me that she shares the buzz that vibrates inside me.

This is Christine's first multiday cycling trip, so she probably has a little trepidation lurking in the corners as well. I have no doubt at all that she'll be fine, what with the consistent and serious walking that she's accustomed to. Fitness is not an issue. While riding a bike is different from walking, she's worked hard to get into shape for this trip. We've spent enough time in the saddle in preparation that I think she knows she can do this, but I see the picayune doubt working on her now and then, the one that always niggles at the back of our brain when we're trying something new and big.

I figure a short break will be nice, so I suggest one of her favorite things. "There's a Starbucks at the next exit—want to pull over and get some coffee?"

"Sure, that sounds good. But I can wait a bit if you want to get one a little later."

"It's another couple hundred miles to the next Starbucks, darlin'. This is western Kansas, remember?"

She laughs. "Then by all means, this is our exit!"

For me, coffee is something strong and black. While I probably taste slight differences between one coffee and the next, they're only small differences, not really preferences. I drink it because I like the ritual of drinking a cup of something hot. Well that, and because I like the buzz.

But Christine has a palate that's far more refined and sensitive than mine. For her, Starbucks is simply better coffee. I contend that there's something she likes about the *idea* of Starbucks as well. The ritual of going there, the feeling of being there. I'm pretty sure it's more than just the coffee; it's the *experience*. And that's perfectly fine—it's an experience I'm learning to enjoy.

I often joke about the time that Starbucks probably saved our relationship from ruin. It happened not long after Christine moved to Colorado, when we were learning to blend with each other. She'd been a walker for years, and I'd ridden bikes for years, so entering into the relationship I knew I'd be walking more to blend with her, and she knew she'd be pedaling more to blend with me.

The early rides we took together were often frustrating for her. While I'd try and find loops from our house that wouldn't be too far, or have too many hills, or have too much traffic, I often failed. I didn't fully appreciate that even if someone was in excellent shape, as Christine was, it would take them time to build the right muscles for cycling and to be accustomed to traffic around them. What seems like a fairly short and easy grade to someone who's ridden for years feels steep and long to someone who's just finding their cycling legs.

One beautiful autumn day we were trying a new loop that I'd found, and were at about mile fifteen of the loop, with another six or eight miles to go before we got home. We were riding along the side of a road that had a pretty limited shoulder, and the traffic was admittedly heavier than I'd hoped. We were making our way up a long but shallow grade, and I'd let myself get too far out in front of Christine again.

I stopped to wait, happy that in only a short distance we'd be off this busy road and back on side roads. As she approached me, I could see she was dripping with frustration. I only wanted to get us this last few hundred yards to the side street. So I started to mount up again as she got close, but she made it very clear that this ride was over.

"Oh no. Don't get back on your bike. I'm done. That's it. I'm not riding any further. This hill is endless and these cars are way too close to me."

I wasn't sure what to say. Stopping didn't seem like an option that was on the table. The ride wasn't over. We weren't home. I opened my mouth to let her know that this busy section was almost over. "But just a little furth—"

"No! Really Neil, I'm done riding!"

By this time, she'd come to a full stop and was off the bike. She looked like she was about to drop the bike there on the side of the road and sit down on the curb. I could tell that my credibility rating at this point hovered somewhere in single digits, and that she wasn't getting back on the bike. My mind was scrambling for options when my eyes fastened on a Starbucks 100 feet further up the road, halfway to the intersection I needed to get her past so the road would improve.

"Oh look," I exclaimed, "a Starbucks!"

Her eyes brightened as they fastened on that friendly green beacon of sweet caffeine, and I was fairly sure my salvation had just revealed itself. I caught her bicycle as she let go of it. "How 'bout we walk up to the Starbucks and get some coffee, and we can decide what we want to do?"

She looked down at her bicycle with disgust, making it plain to me that she was willing to *walk* to the Starbucks, but that I would be dragging both bikes. Which I happily did.

Thirty minutes and one grande iced caramel macchiato later, all was good with the world. I'd assured her that all we had to do was get across the next intersection, and the ride would improve. We only had six or eight miles more to ride to get home.

"ONLY six or eight miles?! Neil, 'six or eight miles' is not something that comes after the word 'ONLY.' That's a long way still, and I'm tired!"

"Can I get you another caramel macchiato, darlin'?"

She laughed, which put my mind to rest. We'd make it through the day, and maybe beyond.

Starbucks. So much more than just a coffee shop.

After that, we started to consider the idea of riding a tandem together. It would at least smooth out the distance and climbing aspects of riding a bit, as our efforts would be combined, and I could learn to be a little more careful about the roads we would ride on. We picked up a used tandem to give it a try—a mid-90s Ibis Easystreet. To bike people, this is a collector's item, but to Christine and me it was simply a used tandem that we could try without spending too much money.

Neither of us held out great hope that riding on the tandem would work that well. My tandem riding had been limited, never enough to feel comfortable. I felt like I could learn it, but I wasn't sure it would work that well for Christine. The whole "control" thing felt like something we'd struggle to get past. Specifically, on a tandem, the person in the front saddle has all the control, and the person in the back saddle relies completely on trust.

Christine likes to have control of things. Not a criticism, just an observation. I'm the same way. I feel most comfortable when I'm driving. In nearly any situation, I take the conn and drive. Which can be good in some situations, but not always. Christine, it seems, is much the same. While she might relinquish the driver's seat to me when we drive, I'm never convinced she likes the idea.

Now, I'm a reasonably safe driver. It's been four or five decades since I was involved in any kind of vehicular dustup. Most folks seem to feel comfortable when I'm behind the wheel. But Christine's Ford Edge didn't have enough handholds for her to grab whenever I was driving a bit differently than she believed I should, and I'm pretty sure that the place on the passenger-side floorboard that would correspond to where the brake would be sustained some serious blunt-force damage from her foot slamming into it whenever she thought I wasn't on the brake fast enough or hard enough. The woman got her daily dose of calisthenics in a 30-minute ride with me behind the wheel, her arms flailing for a safe handhold, her feet pounding the floorboard in front of her.

It's been a real source of adjustment for both of us as we've learned where we each need to give up control to the other person, and where we need to share control. Sharing control is a skill that neither of us needed to do much in our past, so we've never learned to be good at it. We're both the oldest child in our family, and I suspect this struggle is common among couples where both are oldest among siblings.

Which is all preamble to the trepidation I'd felt that she'd be able to enjoy herself in the stoker's saddle of a tandem. Happily, my trepidation was needless, as over the first few dozen rides we settled into a nice symbiotic and peaceful pedaling relationship. Christine was able to ride in the stoker's saddle behind me on the tandem without wild gesticulations trying to redirect my actions as I guided us along the road. We had some learning curves, both on how to ride a tandem well and on how to communicate well, but we survived the curves.

Christine believes that this unexpected comfort with the stoker's saddle is due to the fact that it had been so long since she'd spent much time on a bicycle that she didn't have her own bicycle driving style to compare to mine as we rode, making it easy for her to accept my style as safe and reasonable. That's the best theory I've heard.

The time we spent pedaling the Ibis together taught us that we felt good about this mode of cycling, and that it was something we wanted to continue, expand, and explore. A multiday tour was in our future, and we felt like something relatively easy, flat, and traffic-free would be the ideal starting place. We did a bit of exploring and chose the Katy Trail as our maiden voyage.

While we fit well together as a couple on our Ibis, the captain's cockpit of the frame was way too big for me. We could certainly make the Ibis work for us on the Katy, but it seemed that taking the plunge and buying a new tandem that fit us well would make more sense before the tour than after it. So we spent some time exploring options, and decided on a new Co-Motion Equator.

It's that new Co-Motion Equator that I'm checking on now.

Our Starbucks stop in Colby complete, Christine holds my coffee for me as I crawl into the bed of the truck to check the padding and straps securing the new steed. Satisfied that all is well, I button up the back and hold the passenger door for Christine to climb back in. Firing up the trusty Cummins diesel that's been patiently waiting under the hood of the Dodge, I steer us back onto I-70, where we continue our trek east through a beautiful early autumn day on the prairie.

From Colby headed east, the next real Starbucks is 250 miles down the road in Junction City. There are a couple of "almost" Starbucks outlets tucked into grocery stores along the way (one in Hays and one in Salina), but Christine doesn't really count those except in an emergency. She cradles her Starbucks between her hands, smiling, happy for the cup of comfort. We're good at least until Junction City, and east of there, the Starbucks options open up significantly.

Oh, so much more than just a coffee shop.

~

Late-summer evenings in the Midwest are deep and abiding treasures. We're enjoying this wealth on the front porch of the Main Street Inn Bed & Breakfast in downtown Parkville, Missouri. The sounds of crickets and cicadas serenade us as we gently rock in the old chairs. Rain falls off and on, saturating the air with humidity and encouraging the mosquitos that hover around Christine's bare arms and legs.

She looks over at me with a bemused mixture of jealousy, wonder, and a little anger. While the tiny biting demons swarm around her, gnawing and harassing, I sit, quiet and oblivious. Sometimes I think I understand why the biochemical and thermal differences between Christine and me result in such a stark difference in our attractiveness to mosquitos. It could be that mosquitos clearly enjoy sweet things, and abhor bitter and tough old things. Hence, they swarm to Christine's sweet nature while avoiding the crusty old guy sitting next to her. Although I'm not sure whether my theory holds any water, the difference is center stage on the front porch as Christine swats and slaps ceaselessly at the hungry buggers who seem completely indifferent to the fact that I'm sitting 18 inches away with an exposed bald head and bare arms. I try to show empathy by swatting at imaginary bites now and then, but she usually sees through the sham, which only frustrates her more.

"Stop faking it!" she exclaims.

I sit quietly and try to exude empathy.

"Dinner with Erik and Ellen was nice," she says. My brother and his wife live in Kansas City and had driven out to Parkville to meet us at a local dive. Getting together with them for supper was the primary reason for leaving Colorado early this morning. While Erik and I usually get together to fish a few times during the year, we don't include Christine and Ellen often enough in our socializing.

"Yeah, I love spending time with Erik. Every time I'm with him it reminds me how much I enjoy his company and wish we lived closer."

"You've said before that there's friction between you and Ellen, but I don't ever see it. Are you sure you don't just imagine it? I mean, she seems so nice, and I can't imagine the two of you not getting along."

Ellen and I have had discussions revolving around politics and religion in the past, and they rarely end well. These days, it seems we've agreed to avoid these topics in the interest of good familial relations. She's a lovely person and my brother's wife. My brother loves her, and that love extends from him to me and back to her, no matter what. I suspect she feels the same way.

I have a tendency to be that guy who ends up in arguments over politics and religion. While I consider myself a centrist on most things political, my friends on the right think I lean left, and my friends on the left think I lean right. Which, in my opinion, proves my point. But I can rub people the wrong way because I tend to question everything. I've always felt that it's pretty hard to hold onto an extreme perspective—any extreme perspective—if you're willing to question things and see things from another point of view. So I'm that guy who's constantly needling partners in dialogue with a point of view that contradicts theirs.

This pisses a lot of people off. We don't want our perspectives challenged. We like the comfort of our firmly held biases and prejudices. We've all got 'em, and we don't want somebody else coming in with a different set that messes with the set that we spend a great deal of time and effort cultivating and feeding. We like to listen to news, faux or real, that confirms our bias, reinforcing for us just how right we must be.

There was an awful lot of what my dad said that I ignored, but one of the key things I learned from him and carry with me to this day is the passion he had for challenging biases. He believed that you can't effectively argue a point unless you can effectively argue against the point. It makes perfect sense when you think about it, and it's the basis of that quality in me that can be so irritating to some people—that insistence on everyone understanding all perspectives in an argument.

Not that many people today can have a real discussion and dialogue, a back and forth where both parties learn from the other, and both might actually help the other see another perspective. Most "discussions" today are not much more than sermons—people preaching their own propaganda to one another in an attempt to "convert" their opponent. I'm okay with that, so long as both parties are willing to listen to one another's sermons with real interest.

"No, we get along great these days," I respond to Christine's comment. "Ellen's a wonderful person and I love her dearly. We simply avoid politics and religion in our discussion. Which, really, is probably good advice for many family situations these days."

"I don't know; just because you don't agree on something doesn't mean you can't talk about it, right?"

"I suppose." I stop and think a few seconds before continuing. "Remember tonight when the topic of recent police shootings came up? It was clear that from Erik's and Ellen's perspective, the real issue was the lawlessness and horror of people shooting cops, right?"

"I guess. At least that's what got brought up."

"And discussions you and I have had before have centered around the apparently innocent people—generally people who aren't white—who're killed by police officers and the killings are caught on bystanders' iPhones."

"Right. But we're talking about different things."

"But are we? Don't those things all tie together? I'm not justifying the killing of an unarmed man by a cop, especially in those cases where that unarmed man doesn't appear to have done anything wrong. Nor am I justifying the killing of an innocent cop by some civilian with a gun. Both are wrong. But which one I focus on reveals a little bit about the bias I'm carrying into the discussion, right?"

"Sure, I see your point. But I think you're making more of this than necessary. They were simply expressing horror that cops are being gunned down in cold blood."

"And if I went down into the hood and brought this up, the good folks there would be expressing equal horror at the innocent black men who are being gunned down in cold blood by cops."

"Sure, but why can't I express horror at one or the other without you thinking that it's about bias?"

"If somebody expresses horror over the violence that's building in the country right now, and the senseless killing of black men by cops *and of* cops by black men, then I'm 100% on board, and share in that expression of horror. It's horrific, and finding a solution means seeing the whole problem."

"Neil, you're making too much out of this. Really, they were just expressing sorrow for a bad situation."

"Yeah. Maybe. Bottom line is that I let the comments rest. Or at least I think I did."

"Well, you've clearly got a history that I've not been part of. And I get that you're worried that trying to bring up a different perspective to consider might take things down a nasty rabbit hole."

"Exactly. Which is why we wisely avoid politics and religion."

"Still, you're overthinking it in my opinion. I think you should be more willing to see the good and innocent per*spective*." The word perspective is broken in half with the second half emphasized in concert with a wicked slap of her hand against her calf, smashing a mosquito full of her blood. "Okay, I've had enough!" she says as she gets up and heads inside.

I follow her through the door, knowing she's right, but also knowing that this is the reason I sometimes struggle to find that sweet spot of acceptance and understanding with many people.

~

At breakfast the next morning, Kathy, the innkeeper at the Main Street Inn, is mortified that she hasn't provided a gluten-free breakfast option for Christine. The fault is mine for not advising her when I made the reservation that we needed that option. She pieces something together, but I feel rotten for putting her in this situation.

People often talk about midwesterners like we're all manners and niceness, and in some ways that's true. But in our inability to be good *receivers* of things, we suck. We never want anyone to make a fuss over us, and we're generally not good at getting gifts. We like making a fuss over someone else, and we like *giving* gifts, but we often lack the social grace to let others do for us the way we'd like to do for them.

I remember an early lesson I got in this regard. I was traveling in the South back in the '70s. A friend from back home had asked me to stop by and pay respects to his aunt while I was there, so I did. She took me into her home and fed me lunch, making such a fuss over me that my midwestern sensibilities felt uncomfortable, as if she was doing too much. In the Midwest, a visitor in this situation would be invited in, maybe offered some iced tea, some polite conversation, then they'd head back out the door and we'd get back to work.

But this woman's southern sensibilities were quite different. I was her guest, and she showered me with tea (sweet, of course), little cakes, fancy silver, and china. She had "help," whom she was constantly asking to get me more of this or fetch some of that. Somehow or another I must have protested too much at the lavish attention, and I remember her reaction of genuine hurt. She talked to me like a mother scolding a son, telling me that it was downright rude to come into someone's home and not let them show you hospitality. This was her home, and I was her guest, and by golly she'd teach me the manners that I should have learned as a little boy.

It was then that I realized for the first time that in receiving with genuine gratitude and grace, we're truly giving a gift to the giver. While I've tried to live with that lesson in mind, those stolid midwestern cultural afflictions still rear their head now and then. In this case, by not letting Kathy make a fuss over us and prepare us a breakfast that we could eat, I've deprived her of the joy she'd get if she *felt like* she'd been a wonderful host.

We need to let people make a fuss over us. And we need to learn how to feel thanks for it in our heart.

Kathy tells us that there's a bike trail in Parkville, and that she's heard talk of some other bike trail that will connect to it and go all the way to Saint Louis. This is the first I've heard of this, and I wonder if this will be some connection they'll build to the Katy Trail. I'll discover later that there is at least some truth to this rumor, as some connection to the Kansas City area is being built-out from Windsor along the Katy Trail, though I don't know whether this connection will extend into Parkville.

After breakfast, Christine and I check out of our room, toss our stuff into the truck, and walk downtown into Parkville, which is an old river town working to revitalize that "old town" feel. We wander down one side of Main Street, through a small farmers' market, then meander back up the other side of Main Street. Parkville was built on a hill, running right down to the river floodplain, so the old homes and downtown stretched up the hill have all been spared the ravages of floods.

It's a quaint town that's fun to walk through, our only disappointment being that so many businesses aren't open at 10:30 on a Saturday morning. Christine and I wonder why the shops in town don't have doors flung wide open, inviting people to come in and browse. We end up spending a little money in the few shops that are open, but most of the shops in town are closed, not benefiting from the folks looking in the windows who might have spent money if given the opportunity. Believing as I do in the concept of commerce, I have to believe that shop owners are closed because there isn't profit in opening up, but that doesn't make logical sense to me. There are buyers on the street, with nowhere to buy.

This won't be the last time on this trip that we'll observe this phenomenon of the shuttered downtown, and wonder about it: small towns across Missouri that appear to lack enough commerce for business owners to keep the doors open, yet evidence suggesting that there are buyers who have some money to spend but nowhere to spend it.

I devoted a fair amount of my career to building businesses and running them. I sometimes find it amusing when people who don't have a good understanding of what it takes to make a business profitable proclaim that a certain venture "would make a fortune" or that "someone should go into business doing that because you could hardly go wrong." And I find it heartening when someone throws themselves into a business venture because it's a dream they have or a passion they want to follow. Likewise I then sometimes find it heartbreaking when the dream shatters in financial losses, their passion left cold in the embers of a failed business.

Here I am, strolling down the sidewalk wondering why more businesses aren't open, convinced that just because there's foot traffic on a Saturday morning, that *must* mean that "someone" could make a business successful, when I have no clue what the demographics of the traffic would be all week long, month after month, season after season.

This, too, is a pattern I'll find myself repeating as the week progresses and we make our way across Missouri. I'll catch myself feeling a little put off that there aren't more businesses open in the small towns we pass through, then I'll realize that if there was a living to be made, someone would probably be making it, and I clearly don't have a complete enough picture of the economics and demographics of the small towns we travel through to even have an opinion.

CHAPTER TWO
CLINTON AND THE HAYSLER HOUSE

*I was armed to the teeth with a pitiful little Smith & Wesson's sev-
en-shooter, which carried a ball like a homoeopathic pill, and it took the
whole seven to make a dose for an adult. But I thought it was grand. It
appeared to me to be a dangerous weapon. It only had one fault—you
could not hit anything with it. One of our "conductors" practiced awhile
on a cow with it, and as long as she stood still and behaved herself she
was safe; but as soon as she went to moving about, and he got to shooting
at other things, she came to grief.*

~**Mark Twain**, *Roughing It*

The western terminus of the Katy Trail is a trailhead outside of Clinton. Pulling into the parking lot, we notice a
fella who looks to be in his late 20s climb off his bike and lean
it against his car. We park the truck and wander around the
trailhead, reading the material posted there.

After a few minutes, the young fella comes over and starts
talking to us. Turns out his name is Mitch, and he's a regular
user of the trail. He just rode his mountain bike about ten miles
up the trail and back, making it a nice 20-mile workout for him.
He's full of great information about the trail, since he's a regular user, including more information about that spur that's being built from Windsor toward Kansas City.

To say Mitch is an extrovert would be understating what feels like the obvious to both Christine and me. He's affable, maybe to a fault—one of those people who stretches the boundaries of "sharing" as you talk with them. One of those places where it feels like he walks across that boundary is when he shares with us that he carries a gun.

I'm positive that the mere mention of the word "gun" in this narrative will get most readers scrambling to the political position that we each defend regarding the hot-potato issue of guns in our culture. Christine and I have very different views on guns, and while I don't believe either of us is extreme in our perspective, we do look at it differently. I share this so that the reader may rest assured this will not become a political diatribe defending one position or another, as I believe I understand and sympathize with both perspectives.

As we're talking to Mitch, he proceeds to go into great detail about how prepared he is for bad guys along the Katy Trail. He says he saw a suspicious-looking character walking along the path once, and ever since, he always carries his .357 Mag with him "just in case." We watch him pantomime a make-believe story of someone trying to mess with him, and him pulling out that "little bit o' difference" from where he keeps it in a small holster at the small of his back, and proceeding to blast away at his imagined bad-guy foe.

Christine and I steer the conversation back to discussion of the trail and the route. While Mitch might be a bit socially awkward at understanding boundaries, it could also be that Mitch represents the boundaries of his social universe quite well, and that Christine and I are simply too conservative about sharing our views. This could very well be a "normal" topic of conversation in this part of Missouri. We find a way to end the discussion politely and make our way back to our truck while Mitch packs his bike into his trunk.

"Should we be worried about perverts or thieves on the

trail?" Christine asks with a look of horror on her face. "Are you supposed to carry a gun while you ride this trail?"

"The only people we need to worry about are people like Mitch who have a gun close at hand and are just itching to find a 'bad guy' to confront," I reply. "I mean, anywhere in the world you could be at risk, but I imagine this rural trail through the heartland of America is one of the safest places we could be when it comes to 'bad guys.'"

I mull this over, outwardly brushing our discussion with Mitch off as silly, but inwardly worried that there are people like Mitch wandering around, armed, convinced that they're the "good guys." And I'm sure he is a good and decent man. But my interaction with him makes me question how safe I feel, knowing that he's walking around with a loaded .357 in his holster.

This is really the crux of the gun discussion. I want to retain my right to own a gun and behave responsibly with it, but I also want to be safe from other people behaving irresponsibly with their guns. Should every single person in America carry a gun, to protect themselves from the possibility that someone mistakes them for a bad guy along the trail and decides to aim their .357 at them? Do we then simply accept the likely outcome that gun violence will rise precipitously as a result of all the poor judgment calls that people make under pressure?

It's a complex issue without simple answers. That's the one thing I'm sure about.

Christine gazes down the railbed right-of-way as it dissolves into unkempt undergrowth. The puzzled look on her face reflects the question she asks. "So the trail doesn't start in Clinton, then?"

"I guess not. But I think town is only a couple miles up the road," I answer.

Sure enough, a few curves in the road later and we're in Clinton, and a couple of blocks into Clinton we find the Haysler House Bed and Breakfast Inn. We're early, well before check-in time, so we park the truck and walk a few blocks to the town square that is downtown Clinton.

On our way, we pass a neat old rail station. It's clear that this rail station sits right on the old Katy line, and it's all dressed up and restored. Why on earth, I wonder, does the Katy Trail end a mile or two from this wonderful rail station in the middle of downtown Clinton? People like me and Christine are starting a tour here, and others end a tour here. It's the ideal time to provide some services for people, capture a little commerce, and promote your town in the bargain. While Christine and I decided to stay in the Haysler House in town, spend a bit of money, and make Clinton a "destination," the town doesn't make it easy to do this. In reading accounts of others who use the trail, it seems fairly common for people to simply pack up or drop off at the trailhead, and avoid the town altogether.

It doesn't make sense to me. With the relentless negative economic pressure on small towns across America, why wouldn't the merchants in Clinton want to participate in the great potential for commerce that pulls in and out of that parking lot outside of town? Month after month, year after year, how many cyclists *don't* come to downtown Clinton and spend money because the trailhead isn't here in downtown where it would have so much more value to the town itself?

The town square in Clinton is beautiful and well maintained. We wander the square, buying a few presents to take home, enjoying some coffee, soaking up a beautiful September day in the Midwest. We hadn't really planned on eating supper, but a couple of places look like interesting supper options, and we consider whether to come back down to the square after we get checked in, to enjoy the local cuisine. Coffee'd up, our anticipation and excitement for our coming trip growing, we head back to the Haysler House to check in.

Roger greets us at the door with a glass of sherry and shows us around the place. He's a wealth of information about the house itself, the details behind individual components that went into the building of it, and the political history of the family who commissioned it. Christine and I both love history, so we're captivated by the stories that Roger shares with us.

After a quick shower, we decide local cuisine sounds good, so we head back into town for an early supper at one of the local places that looked interesting earlier. It's Saturday, and it turns out that sometimes on Saturday evenings, the town hosts a car show, where car buffs from around the area drive their restored classics into town and park them around the square. Folks walk up and down the lines of old cars, admiring them, chatting with the owners.

We observe a few different kinds of folks admiring the old machines. There are the old geezers like me for whom many of these old classics bring back memories of our youth. There's a beautiful old '56 Chevy that's been lovingly restored, which stirs recollection of a good friend who spent all his time and money restoring a similar machine. Of course, in my memory, that old car melts itself into my image of me as a teenager, and the resulting story is something more grand than the real life that happened. The truth is that I, like most guys I knew, drove old junk heaps when we were teenagers. Held together with baling wire and duct tape, those old jalopies represented our independence and our manhood, and they were all we could afford on the $1.60 per hour we earned, which was the minimum wage at the time.

There are also quite a few young folks arrayed around the square taking in the old cars. To them, these heaps of metal are relics of a time they don't remember, and the look on their faces is more amazement than remembrance. The $1.60 an hour we earned as minimum wage in the late '60s would sound like an astonishingly low wage to them; but when adjusted for inflation, it was the highest the minimum wage has ever been, before or since—50 percent higher than the last minimum wage increase when it was implemented in 2009.

And then, there are the wives of us old mossbacks. Christine walks with me, holding my hand, trying hard to muster some interest in these ancient heirlooms that hold so much fascination to me. But her attention strays often to the bandstand where some more old fogies are setting up to start playing a little music, or maybe to the café where some nachos and a margarita might be calling her name.

We eventually make it over to that diner on the corner and enjoy a couple of margaritas with a light supper. We make fun of ourselves and of our fascination with all this nostalgia. We realize that while we might fit into the age demographic of the majority of people wandering around the square and eating supper in the cantina, we don't fit the recreational demographic. While it's impossible to know for sure, we don't see anyone else around us who gives us the outward or obvious impression that they're here as a cyclist.

Our conversation circles back to where it was earlier today, wondering why there aren't more cyclists wandering around, enjoying the beautiful old town square, contributing to the commercial health of the town. A mile away, the trailhead parking lot sits, quiet, full of lonely cars patiently waiting for their drivers to return. If all those cars were parked here in town instead of a mile away, some portion of their drivers might walk through the café door and have supper. Not only on Saturday night when a car show is going on, but maybe, eventually, every single day. As it is, it's just me and Christine who bucked the trend and decided to stay in town and spend a few dollars here.

I take one last glance at the old machines as we walk out the door of the café, paying my respects to an era gone by. Or is it nostalgia for my youth? A youth that I again realize was probably far less marvelous than the one my memory has created.

~

Breakfast at the Haysler House Sunday morning is nothing short of spectacular. Roger, it seems, is quite the chef. Christine and I immediately regret that we didn't take Roger up on his offer to prepare supper for us last night.

Since we have 70+ miles to ride today, we want to get an early start, and Roger graciously accommodates our request for an early breakfast. Our gear packed onto our bike, our driving clothes stowed in the back of the truck, we sit down to Roger's culinary delight while he and Annette assure that no corner of our appetite goes unsatisfied.

Breakfast complete, the truck parked out of the way, Roger snaps the obligatory start-of-the-trip picture for me with my camera, and Christine and I hit "Start" on both the Garmin and the GoPro and head off through the streets of Clinton toward that place a mile from town where the Katy Trail begins.

A mile from town. Really. Why not actually finish the project?

FOOTNOTE: A little research later will reveal that when the trail was being conceived and designed, there was some thought given to establishing the trailhead right there at that wonderful rail station, creating a perfect destination that would draw cyclists to downtown Clinton. One person I talked to said that when the trail was being built, there was political resistance from a few influential people to the idea that the town would need to financially participate in the construction of the final mile into town. Their refusal to help fund that final mile resulted in the trailhead being located a mile or so from town. Now I can't report any of this as factual, but only as hearsay based on the small bit of asking that I did. The bottom line is that I believe there are probably an awful lot of cyclists using the trail who end up *not* spending time and money in downtown Clinton because the trailhead is outside of town rather than downtown, and the decision to let that happen may very well have been penny wise and pound foolish.

CHAPTER THREE
CLINTON TO BOONVILLE

There comes a time in every rightly-constructed boy's life when he has a raging desire to go somewhere and dig for hidden treasure.
~ **Mark Twain**, *The Adventures of Tom Sawyer*

The air is thick with fog as we glide through the empty streets of Clinton, our first pedal strokes of the trip filled with shared excitement as we make our way to the trailhead. Once there, we stop and turn off our lights, taking pictures of beautiful webs hanging heavy with moisture, shining brightly with the hidden sunlight that works hard to penetrate the dense fog from somewhere in front of us.

Pedaling again, I find it impossible to ride with glasses on, a nonstop stream of dew sweating across them as we roll through the thick mist, with visibility at maybe 50 feet. The muffled crunch of our tires is the only sound we hear as we spin across the finely crushed stone that surfaces the trail. It's a spectacularly beautiful morning that we're winding through, wet webs shimmering in the trees that line the trail, early- morning light soft and warm as it seeps through the thick cloud that rests on the shoulders of the eastern Missouri farmland we cruise across.

As the fog slowly melts away, we see the landscape around us alternate between woods and field. The wooded sections are generally early growth deciduous woodland, young trees that hang over the trail and create a canopy, the roof of a tunnel pierced by the trail. The open sections usually have cultivated field on one side, commonly late-season beans but interspersed with occasional corn stubble or alfalfa. Rich scents saturate the air around these fields, sometimes lush and verdant, often damp and stagnant, occasionally sharp and dry.

We stop beside a tractor that rests close to the trail, climbing off the bike and walking through the grass to take a few pictures. Our two-year-old grandson is enthralled with anything machine-like or tool-like, and we figure taking selfies with the tractors will be a fun thing to send him as we progress across the state. This early-morning selfie in front of a bright green John Deere dripping with morning dew is the first in a series of tractor selfies.

My shoes squish beneath me, already wet from the saturated air and now waterlogged from the little stroll through the grass for the John Deere selfie. I wipe the newly collected dew from my saddle before climbing back on, astonished at how much moisture is falling out of the air even as the sun struggles to claw its way through the haze.

While the wet air is a bit of an annoyance, neither of us complain. We live in Colorado, where the air is extremely dry, and spending time with all this rich wet air moving through our sinuses and lungs feels wonderful to us.

As we bring the bike up to speed and find our pedaling rhythm again, Christine suggests that a Starbucks would be nice about now. We chuckle at this, both realizing that we're not likely to find a Starbucks, but we might find a coffee shop in one of the towns up ahead. While any coffee shop we find might do, anything less than Starbucks is, well, something less than Starbucks.

Christine has taught me to be much more civilized as a cyclist. When we ride together on the tandem around town in Denver, we often identify a Starbucks as the destination for our ride. This *destination cycling* was new to me, and I quickly learned that it enhanced our mutual enjoyment when we rode. For me, and for buddies with whom I'd ridden for years, water bottles were the thing you used to hydrate yourself, and a granola bar in your jersey pocket was how you got a few calories as you rode. Hydrate as you ride, though now and then you might stop and lean against the bike as you eat a granola bar. On a particularly long and hard ride, say an 80-mile loop with climbing, maybe we'd try and plan a place to stop and have brunch or lunch as a treat.

The idea of stopping for coffee as part of most bike rides was foreign to me. It never entered my mind. If someone had asked me about stopping at a Starbucks for coffee, my answer would probably have been something like, "If I'm thirsty I have a water bottle, I drank coffee before we left, and why would I take time out of my ride to sit in a coffee shop?"

But I've evolved since those days as a primitive creature. I've learned that maximum enjoyment of a ride happens when it starts out with a conversation about where we'll be stopping and enjoying a cup of coffee. Instead of describing a ride as a nice 50-mile loop around town, as I might have done previously (in my days as a cretin), I now describe that same ride as a nice ride downtown for coffee on Larimer Square, then a ride back along Cherry Creek, with maybe another stop at the Starbucks that we'll pass along the way if we want to. Same ride, wayyyy more mutual enjoyment.

This morning, riding on the Katy, Christine clearly has something like this in mind. In her ride calculations, our 70 miles or so of riding today will surely include not only a lunch stop, but a couple of coffee stops as well. And frankly, my evolved sensibilities find this notion appealing.

We look around as we ride through Calhoun, seeing no coffee shop. There may be a diner somewhere that we can't see from the trail. While this would be a great time for a coffee stop, we're okay with putting a few more miles in with the hope of finding a stop in the next town.

Eight miles up the road, all we see is a Casey's convenience store as we roll through Windsor. Christine is not happy. I remember seeing a scene from The Man with the Golden Arm, where the character that Frank Sinatra plays contemplated the possibility that he might have to go without heroin. The look on Christine's face as she contemplates the possibility that there might not be a coffee shop along the trail reminds me of the look Sinatra had in his eyes in the movie.

"We're not likely to find a real coffee shop here, are we?" she asks.

"I don't think so darlin', but if we ride through town we might find a diner or something where we could sit down for coffee."

I see her thinking about this as she looks at the little convenience store, sadness in her eyes. It's hard to watch your mate's hopes dashed against the damp crushed rock of a bicycle trail. While it's clear that she'd accept stopping at Casey's for coffee, I'm hopeful that maybe in the next town there'll be a diner where we can sit and sip coffee, and so I suggest we keep pedaling. Maybe we can't find her Starbucks dream, but if we're lucky, perhaps a bit more of a reverie than sitting on the concrete sidewalk of a gas station.

Nine miles later we roll through Green Ridge, and we've come to terms with the reality that convenience store coffee is probably all we're going to get. Without hesitation she suggests we pedal the couple hundred yards over to the Casey's north of the crossing. We grab a snack and a coffee and mosey on over to the city park next door, where we sit at a picnic table and savor our treat. It's not Starbucks, but it's coffee, and it's quite pleasant sipping coffee in the quiet small-town park, watching the last of the early-morning mist burn away around us. I breathe a sigh of contentment knowing that my wife is just a little bit happier now.

Sedalia is a fairly big town where I feel certain we'll be able to find a decent place to have lunch. Back in 2012 I connected with the Katy Trail in Sedalia, and my assumption based on my 2012 experience has been that the trail itself actually winds along city streets. While this is true, the "gap" in the trail where we are forced off the trail and onto streets for a while doesn't happen until you've passed most of the town itself, and by then you're well beyond any part of town where you'll find a place to eat lunch.

Better planning on my part would have been nice. As it is, we end up doing a bit of backtracking and add several extra miles to our day. We find a Hardee's where we sit and enjoy milkshakes, sodas, burgers, and fries. We have some fun conversations with a counter clerk who's about our age and wishing she and her husband would have an adventure like we're having.

Vicariousness. I see someone having some adventure, and I like putting myself in their shoes, dreaming about what it would be like to have that adventure. This woman believes she'd like to get her husband to ride a tandem with her along the Katy Trail, and who am I to judge how much she truly wants this to happen or what the possibility is that she could actually talk her husband into joining her? But right now, looking at us and at our bike, she's dreaming of how much she thinks she'd like to have this adventure, and I'm delighted that we're able to help her have that dream.

I wonder if this is how most big transformations in life are conceived. We see some adventure, or some new situation or trail to explore, and we envision ourselves in that situation or exploring along that trail. Christine and I are in the early phases of one of those types of envisioning exercises right now in life, wondering if retiring to a sailboat to explore the world would be a thing that we'd enjoy in retirement, which is rapidly approaching. I have no idea if it would be good for us or not, but we've learned a bit, and every couple we see living on a sailboat helps us to form the picture in our mind of what it would look like to have that adventure in our life.

We backtrack and explore our way through Sedalia streets and rejoin the Katy Trail. I should mention that when Christine and I are traveling together and I use the term "explore," it usually elicits a bit of apprehension from her. This is because of a wide disparity between us when it comes to our natural sense of direction.

For whatever reason, I'm lucky to have a decent navigational sense. My friend Glenn Gustavson used to say I have a good sense of "dead reckoning." (Turns out that's a sailing term, which I should have guessed, since Glenn is a sailor.) I enjoy getting just a little lost and then finding my way in new places. It becomes a puzzle game to me, as I scroll through the map that's coming together in my mind to help me see where I am. Not that I never get lost, because I do. But even when I do get lost, it's fun looking for ways to get un-lost.

Which I often call "exploring." Christine will ask me if I know where I am, and my answer is often the word "mostly," which makes perfect sense to me. It means I know roughly or mostly where I am on the map that my little brain is constructing, and that I'm looking for clues that will home me in on exactly where I am.

But to Christine, this is equivalent to being lost. In Christine's world, she either knows exactly where she is, or she's lost. She builds landmarks in her brain that define things for her in a very verbal sense. "I always turn right by the red house," or

"Just past the mailbox that's under the pine tree is where I turn left." So if the mailbox or the red house or the pine tree aren't where she thinks they should be, then she's lost.

It doesn't help that she (like most women) has had her share of experiences throughout life with fellow humans who happen to carry a Y chromosome, genetically predisposing them to difficulty in asking for directions. As scientists have long been aware, the existence of a Y chromosome in a human usually makes him incapable of asking for directions. It also severely limits his capacity for vocabulary, causing him to tend toward grunts as a typical response to questions. It also causes him to be born a male.

Against these great odds, she's learned to trust my navigational good fortune over the years we've been together. Still, I always sense a tiny bit of panic when she hears me say that I know *mostly* where we are, and that I'm *exploring*.

After a few miles of this exploring, we find ourselves at that spot on the northeast side of town, along Boonville Street, where the trail takes off to the left. I recognize the spot immediately as the place where I picked the trail up back in 2012.

The trail throughout the day has had more up and down to it than I expected, a tendency that continues along this section east of Sedalia. Even though we're now about halfway through our day, the section after Sedalia feels much longer to us than the morning section did, which I'm sure has something to do with the fact that it's turned into a hot September day. It's 30 miles from where we fill our water bottles in Sedalia to Pilot Grove, which is the first place we find along the trail that has any supplies. It's a long 30 miles in the heat, and by the time we get there, we're both ready for today's ride to be over. Knowing we have another 12 miles to go, we spend some extra time hydrating on the sidewalk outside the Casey's convenience store not far from the trail.

When we're ready to leave, Christine goes back inside to use the restroom, and I roll the bike over to where a fella has a brand-new Harley he's leaning on while his wife is inside. They only bought the bike a couple of days ago, and her maiden voyage has them headed to Boonville for an overnight. We chat a bit as we wait for our wives, and I have to admit to doing a bit of vicarious fantasizing myself, seeing this beautiful new motorcycle all decked out with creature comforts, not to mention about 100 horsepower powering the two wheels, against the 0.5 hp that Christine and I probably produce to power our tandem down the trail.

When Christine comes back out, I've got the tandem ready for her to climb on. I bid adieu to my new motorcycle friend and head back to the trail. Once rolling along, Christine proceeds to tell me about her less-than-cordial encounter in the restroom at the Casey's. Seems she'd gone into the one restroom they had, locked the door, and was getting ready to do what one does in the restroom, when a man began pounding on the door, telling her to hurry up. Now, her total time in the Casey's was about what I would expect for most folks to take care of the business one takes care of in a restroom. Two minutes? Three, maybe? At any rate, she did hurry a bit, figuring that the guy must really need to use the restroom. Hands washed, she unlocked the door to leave, and a big smelly guy, dramatically overweight, pushed past her, knocking her to the side with no apology whatsoever, then slammed the door on her.

She tells me this story as we're pedaling along the trail, and that stupid male thing wraps itself around me. Most men reading these words knows the thing I'm talking about. It's some combination of male ego, male protector mode, and unreasonable crusader-for-justice fantasies. It pumps us full of adrenaline, forcing any logic or common sense out of our brains. In this case, some fat jerk pushed my wife, and by god he needs a manners lesson. It's all I can do not to turn the bike around and go be all pushy and shove-y and juvenile with this guy. Break his nose and a few teeth, crack a rib maybe. Teach him a lesson, by golly!

What is it in the typical male that makes us like this? I'm 62 years old, and this big ol' fella is probably half my age, twice my weight, surrounded by friends, and if Mitch back in Clinton was any example, carrying a *bit o' difference* in a holster somewhere. And yet, I find myself talking me down from this irrational urge for retribution.

Christine's unhappy sigh brings me back to the real here and now, where the day is beginning to feel endless. I started the day off with an expectation that our riding would be complete for the day at about 70 miles, an expectation that I'd shared with Christine. Thanks to our wayward meandering through Sedalia as we searched for lunch, we're already past 70 miles for the day and still not in Boonville, and I'm delighted when we finally cross the bridge over I-70 and optimistic to feel the trail tilt down ever so slightly. I risk the hopeful expectation that the trail should keep dropping now for these last few miles into Boonville, and I'm relieved when that prediction actually pans out.

Several times today, I've felt myself sharing a common *sense of being* with Christine. Not all the time, but several times. It's nothing either of us says, but when it happens, I feel quite certain that we're sharing a common feeling. I suppose all relationships are like that as you get to know each other better, and I smile as I realize that what we're sharing right now, cranking these last pedal strokes of a very long day, is something like euphoria. Pleasure, maybe a bit of pride, with a hard day successfully ridden.

Not that there weren't moments of frustration today, or other less-than-pleasant emotions, but those all seem to wash away from us as we glide down this shaded path through beautiful woodland, enjoying the air moving across as we descend, air that cools us now but felt hot just a few miles back. It's amazing the difference a little thing like cresting a hill can make on the way we feel.

I'm a happy man, and I feel my happy bride smiling as we share the final pedal strokes of the day.

CHAPTER FOUR

BOONVILLE AND THE HIGH STREET VICTORIAN HOUSE

I turned in and slept like a log--I don't mean a brisk, fresh, green log, but an old dead, soggy rotten one, that never turns over or gives a yelp.
~ **Mark Twain**, *Letter to Olivia Clemens, December 16, 1871*

We roll up to the High Street Victorian House Bed & Breakfast and find innkeeper Kriss reading a book on the front porch, waiting for us to arrive. We dismount, and she and Gene come out to the sidewalk and help us move our bike to the backyard, lock it up, and carry our gear up to our room.

At the top of the stairs, Kriss points out a plate of cookies and a sideboard of beverages that she's set out for us, emphasizing that they're gluten-free. Christine and I both grab a cookie as we pass, seeing no need whatsoever to be asked twice.

I'm often asked about camping versus staying in hotels when touring on a bike. While I'm not a zealot for or against one style of touring or another, at that point every day when I'm enjoying a warm shower, I'm glad to have lodging. Today is no exception, and I delight in the sweet indulgence of hot water pouring over me, leaching weariness from my muscles as it washes the trail grime away. Feeling civilized again, we wander downtown to enjoy Boonville.

Boonville has become a gambling town. Apparently, in Mis-

souri gambling is legal on riverboats along the Mississippi and
Missouri rivers, and since Boonville is a river town along the
Missouri River, the town has embraced riverboat gambling,
with a large casino complex "floating" where the town meets
the river. When planning this trip, I considered staying at the
casino hotel, but opted instead for a locally owned bed and
breakfast. (My bias for small and locally owned business shines
brightly.)

Strolling along downtown streets in search of supper, we notice the Palace restaurant on the corner of Main Street and
Morgan Street. The unassuming entrance makes it easy to walk
past, but we decide to give it a try. Inside, the decor is decades
old, with plastic chairs and plastic covers on the tables. The
place drips with the kind of class that only exists in old diners.

My kind of place.

The server is a friendly young gal who knows the menu well.
After she takes our order and our drinks arrive, I listen as she
interacts with a group of two couples at the table next to us.
They've obviously been drinking a bit and, based on the questions they ask, are not from here. Within a few minutes, a man
walks up to their table and introduces himself as George, the
proprietor.

Listening to their conversation, I gather that the server is
George's daughter. I can't help but feel like George has come
to the table and inserted himself as a very friendly but strong
reminder that things should remain polite and civil. He talks
with them for quite a while, answering questions, kidding and
having fun, helping them see the limits in a way that only bar-
tenders and restaurant managers can do. An insight and a skill
honed through years of managing drinking folks through their
self-induced drift from the generally accepted norms of social
interaction.

They've wandered off the casino riverboat in search of a local place to eat. The piece of the conversation that strikes me is their question to George about how much he feels like the casino helps his business, what with all the people it must pull into town. It seems to me that they have a clear preconceived notion that surely the casino brings business to town, and the only question is how much business. I think I probably hold the same preconceived notion. It seems to be one of the benefits that local economies are told to expect when gambling meccas are being planned or considered.

They're as surprised by George's answer as I am. He's owned the Palace for many years, since before the casino opened. He says that yes, local merchants probably did have the expectation of increased business as a result of the influx of people into town, but that he feels like the casino has—if anything—hurt his business somewhat. While I can't catch the entire conversation, or all of the ins and outs of why he feels this way, the observation itself makes me pause.

How can this be? All over the country, big enterprises like football stadium owners and casino companies often proclaim wonderful benefits that a community will receive if the community will only provide tax breaks or other giveaways as incentives for the stadium owners or casino companies to open their enterprise in that community. Throngs of people will come to enjoy the enterprise, and small businesses in the area will enjoy wonderful new revenue opportunities. On a much different scale, this is similar to my assumption that the town of Clinton would benefit from a trailhead downtown rather than a trailhead a mile from town.

Yet, this business owner doesn't believe the casino has helped his business at all and in fact has probably hurt it. His belief is that few of the people who are attracted to the casino are going to want to leave the casino to go eat supper in a small town. They've come for the casino, and that's where they'll spend their money. The town might benefit from extra tax income eventually, depending on how the tax incentives are structured, and surely there will be a few businesses in town who will benefit, but he doesn't believe that he's seen it.

The conversation makes me question my earlier assumptions about the likely commercial benefits of extending the Katy Trail into downtown Clinton. It seems to me that my assumptions are still valid, but it also causes me to realize that it's easy to sell ourselves on the "obvious" benefits that we're likely to realize from courses of action that we're already predisposed to be in favor of.

It also brings to light a likely reticence that small-town leaders might have toward notions that outsiders bring to them about growth opportunities in their town. If they've believed the hype before and have built expectations on it, and the expectations fail to materialize, then they're probably pretty likely to be very cautious the next time someone suggests a "great opportunity" for their town. Could it be that trail promoters ran into this when trying to get the trail extended into downtown Clinton?

Our food arrives, and my attention wanders away from the conversation George is having. It's not spectacular food, but simple food done extremely well. And there are few things in life better than something simple done well.

I know that my enjoyment of a thing is often tightly coupled to how much I need the thing, much like my enjoyment of a shower earlier was enhanced by the fact that I desperately needed to wash grime from my skin and feel hot water bathe my sore muscles. Without a doubt, my body needs food right now, and surely this enhances my enjoyment of supper, but even considering this, Christine and I feel like we've hit the jackpot at our simple little table at the Palace.

Back at our B&B, it takes us only moments to fall into deep sleep on a sinfully comfortable mattress, the cool September breeze caressing its way through the room. Remember, dear reader, that a shower was the one time that I am *always* glad to have paid for lodging after a day of cycling? Nights of sleep like we experience at the High Street Victorian Bed & Breakfast come in a close second.

CHAPTER FIVE
BOONVILLE TO JEFFERSON CITY

Grief can take care of itself; but to get the full value of a joy you must have somebody to divide it with.

~ **Mark Twain**, *Following the Equator*

Without thinking about it, we started a tradition yesterday. We took a selfie early in the day, when we were feeling optimistic, spunky, and strong. At Pilot Grove we were feeling a bit more pessimistic, a little less strong, and the last hint of spunk abandoned us somewhere north of Sedalia. At that point, I'd taken another selfie, over the protests of my bride.

This morning, we decide we should continue the tradition—a before and after picture for every day. Standing in front of the High Street Victorian House Bed & Breakfast, we snap another selfie. The day is young and bright, with less than 60 miles planned for the day, and Christine shares a warm and loving kiss on the cheek as an expression of optimism.

We ride across the Missouri River on a superb bike lane that's completely separated from the car traffic on the bridge, stopping to take pictures a few times. Christine asks me if we're likely to run across a Starbucks today, and I reply that while I'm pretty sure we won't, I'm also confident that we'll be able to find a coffee shop in Rocheport. I remind her that Rocheport is the small town where we stopped back in 2013 when we were driving across Missouri as she was moving out to Colorado. She smiles, content that her morning will be made complete by that wonderful warm latte, probably enjoyed at a table sitting outside the little coffee shop we both remember.

Yesterday the trail trundled through farmland, undulating with the roll of the land. Within a few miles this morning, it's clear that we've left the rolling farmland behind, and that the trail has dropped into the floodplain of the Missouri River.

Flat. As a pancake. The only elevation changes occur at bridges, where the trail might pitch up a few feet, cross the bridge, then drop right back down to that wonderful supine plane. It's truly wonderful riding, the trail ducking in and out of forest, oftentimes with farmland on one side or the other. We find a gear we like, and crank through the miles.

Now and then there are washouts along the trail, a result of water washed across the trail during recent heavy rains. It's mildly irritating, because these places are hard to pick out among the shadows cast across the trail from the sun shining through the trees above. I don't recall any of this at all when I rode the trail four years ago, so I assume it must be an isolated problem.

About 13 miles into our day, the trail dives into a fanciful tunnel that leads us shortly out into the quaint little town of Rocheport. I hear a delighted exclamation from Christine as she recognizes the place where we strolled along only a few years back, talking about the possibility that maybe we could ride this trail together someday.

We're both anticipating a cup of coffee outside the coffee shop we remember, reminiscing over the journey we've shared over the last few years, and how far we've come to end up back here. As we roll up to the building where we remember the coffee shop, we're greeted by another cyclist with bad news. "The place looks to be closed permanently," he says sadly as he sits on a picnic bench.

"What?!" Christine exclaims. "That can't be." We stop the bike and look around. Christine climbs off the saddle and walks over to the building to validate for herself. Still in disbelief, she plops down on the picnic bench opposite the dejected fella (who introduces himself as James), the two of them consumed by the sadness of anticipation deprived, kindred souls lost together in a sense of unfulfilled craving for a cup o' joe.

I glance around, looking for a gas station or something, and spot a couple of gals on bikes rolling toward us with the same look of deprivation that Christine and her new Starbucks soul mate are displaying. They look like they might be sisters.

"You gals been looking for a coffee shop?" I ask.

"We can't find anything in town anywhere," the older one answers, as the younger looks longingly at the locked door of the erstwhile coffee shop by the trail. "Somebody told us there's a place to get coffee further up the trail in McBaine. But I need coffee now!"

Christine and James catch this comment, and their shoulders slump with defeat. I realize that I've been looking forward to enjoying coffee in the morning sunshine as well, and I share a bit of the disappointment that I feel from them. Hopefully we'll find a place further up the road where we can enjoy coffee, but I'm not optimistic, as this is the largest town we'll see this morning.

Looking from face to face within our little group here outside a closed coffee shop, I realize that we may all share a common flaw in our planning and expectations regarding riding along the trail. It may be that we've all ridden other rail trails, or this rail trail for that matter, on weekends or later in the week, and that we've come to expect to find things like coffee shops along the way catering to cyclists. And really, on the weekends, we'd

likely find more of it. Right now, here are five of us sitting outside a closed coffee shop, and during our few minutes of com-
miserating at the picnic bench, we'll watch a few other folks
cycle past along the trail.

But is that enough business for an entrepreneur to make a
living? It's easy for me to assume so, but what do I know about
the economics of running a small business in a small town in
the middle of Missouri? Rocheport is the quintessential Missouri river town. It's quaint and cute in all the ways that make
for a great tourist destination. The town has done what feels to
me like an excellent job of investing in the trail as a destination
within the town. And really, I've been here on other days when
the town was bustling with tourists, and these picnic benches
outside the coffee shop were packed with people.

And yet, this business has a sign on the door saying that it's
closed permanently. I'll discover in several days during our
shuttle ride back to Clinton from Alton that the fella who owns
this little shop has recently been stricken by some serious med-
ical issues, and that's what's caused him to close his shop. But
standing over my bike here this morning, soaking up the caf-
feine-craving despondency around me, I struggle to understand
the economics.

As I type these words in 2017, my highly competent and
tireless research assistant (who goes by the name of Google)
informs me that a young couple (Brandon and Whitney Vair)
have opened the Meriwether Café and Bike Shop right along
the trail in town. Their website says they're open 7:00 a.m. until
sunset six days a week, closed on Mondays, and that they even
rent bikes. While I'm not here to plug their business for them, I
don't want to leave readers with the impression that they might
have the same caffeine-impoverished experience that Christine
and I had in Rocheport.

Which is, for me, a happy ending to this little sub-story. Here in the quintessential Missouri River town of Rocheport it appears that there is, indeed, an economy bolstered by the cycling community in a way that may well support an endeavor like a coffee shop or café. Brandon and Whitney seem to be strengthening their odds of success by merging the café with a bike shop.

Rural isolation is one of the true beauties of the Katy Trail. It is strikingly provincial from end to end. With that beauty comes the balance of less convenience. It's Monday, and riders along the trail on Monday should expect to find most businesses closed. That's just the way of it. The outrage that we all share here at the picnic table seems like a symptom of our over-commercialized social culture, where I expect that if I'm a paying customer with money to spend, a merchant should be standing by, providing me with a place to spend my money.

Had I planned this journey well, knowing how much we like to stop and enjoy coffee in the middle of the morning, I would have included a Thermos as part of our essential equipment, and would have filled the Thermos with hot coffee before we climbed on the bike in the morning. Then we could have found an idyllic little spot each morning to enjoy our coffee.

Christine trudges back over to where I'm still standing over the bike, and climbs on the back. I share my pessimism about coffee in our future this morning, and feel despondency drip from the air around me as we roll back onto the bike path headed east out of Rocheport.

Sometimes, a cup of coffee is oh so much more than just a cup of coffee …

The trail east of Rocheport is stunning. A canopy of forest creates a beautiful tunnel through which we glide, openings in the canopy revealing the Missouri River stretching across the flood plain on our right, limestone cliffs towering above on our left. If you were putting together a list of the sections of trail not to miss, this section would be high on the list. Right after passing the Huntsdale milestone, the trail crosses farmland for a few miles before plunging back into the cool and shady woodland along the river.

There are several side trails we notice as we ride, some of them marked with signs indicating that the trail might take you to a winery. How cool would it be if these wineries also provided lodging? That way, riders could plan on riding from winery to winery, stopping each day and enjoying wine. If it was later in the day, a side trip and a glass of wine might be fun. But then, the vineyards are likely high on the hills to our left, so how many cyclists would want that sort of climb? Would there be enough traffic along the trail to justify some sort of shuttle or other presence along the trail that would make an ideal like that feasible? I mention these thoughts to Christine as they rattle around in my tiny brain, and I am reminded that it's coffee we need to find, not wine, and that while the winery signs are cute, it's a green Starbucks sign that would light up her life right now.

We hit McBaine and discover no coffee shop or convenience store, or anything that looks like a source of java. The trail crosses a road, and a building off to the right 500 feet or so doesn't look like a store, certainly not a coffee shop. If anything, it looks like it might be a bar and grill. After a brief rest at the McBaine trailhead, we clip into the pedals and continue east.

The next six or seven miles continue the beautiful tunnel through the forest, the trail well maintained and in good shape. We've seen quite a few snakes along the trail this morning, usually black snakes, but across this section we have a close encounter with a copperhead. It blends so well with the trail that I don't see it until the last minute, swerving slightly to avoid running over it. By pure luck it's the tail side of the snake rather than the head side that we swerve past, preventing any possible attempt at a strike by the little fella.

We break out of the woodlands we've been rambling through and see Cooper's Landing marina on our right. We pull over, lean our bike against a picnic table, and order coffee from the small general store and diner that's part of the marina. Cooper's Landing is a real oasis for us today, and we're grateful that it's here and open.

As we're mounting back up, we realize we forgot something back at the McBaine trailhead, so we backtrack the six or seven miles, then ride it again. I watch for our copperhead trail companion, and my feelings aren't hurt a bit when I see that he's apparently abandoned the trail. We pass Cooper's Landing a second time with an extra dozen or so miles logged for the day. I promised Christine an easy day with less than sixty miles of riding, and I see that promise evaporating into a cloud of wishes.

From Cooper's Landing to Hartsburg is about a dozen miles. Cool forest rises on our left through these miles, and to our right we see occasionally the broad width of river, and at other times it's rich farmland stretched across the floodplain. The washed-out sections of the trail seem much worse in these sections where there is farmland around us, and they've been getting worse as we've progressed east. There are occasional sections where Christine opts to get off the bike while I ride around or through the ruts.

It's late in the day when we ride into Hartsburg and take a brief spin around town (two or three spins around town would still be brief) and confirm that nothing is open. In 2012 I spent the night at the Globe Hotel in Hartsburg as I traveled across the country, and I wrote about the town, the bed and breakfast, and the proprietor in *Pilgrim Spokes*. The bed and breakfast was now run by new proprietors, but I still wanted to drop off a copy of the book for them. So we wheel up to the Globe and knock on the door, introducing ourselves to the new owners. Leaia and Mark are a delightful and energetic young couple. They're very gracious and fill our water bottles with ice and water while we chat, a kindness greatly appreciated as we're hot and tired, and our water bottles are empty. After a few minutes of friendly chat, we make our way back to the trail to continue our trek toward Jefferson City.

Only a few miles have passed when the trail disappears into a flooded field. A creek seems to be flooded, and the water is high enough that it swallows the trail. This is about as washed out as you can get. We consider riding through it, or carrying the bike and walking through it, but from where we stand we can't even see the end of the flooded section. We have no idea how deep it might get, or what the trail is like beneath the water. The plethora of snakes we've passed along the trail today conjure up images in Christine's mind of slithery things unseen beneath the surface, waiting just for her.

Clearly, we'll not be walking through the water. Instead, we backtrack to the last road we passed. Fortunately we have cell reception, so we take a look at Google Maps to see if this road will eventually connect us to roads that will take us to Jefferson City, where we have a reservation for the night. It does, so I commit the route to memory, and we head up the road.

It's less than a mile until the phrase "heading up the road" takes on a much more literal meaning. The road we're on tilts up. Very steeply. It's a gravel road, but the hill is paved. I assume the reason the hill is paved is because it's so steep that they have no other way to keep the erosion at bay. It's about three miles of this sort of rugged, steep up-and-down riding until we find ourselves at US-63, which I know will take us into Jefferson City.

US-63 has a wide shoulder for us to ride on, but the traffic is extremely heavy, and the drivers don't go out of their way to be courteous. The road is never flat, tilting constantly up or down, but the grade is reasonable. If it weren't for the traffic, this would be a nice section of road to ride.

I know that many folks who tour on bicycles opt for busier roads like this, reasoning that the big shoulder adds a level of safety and is worth the trade-off for the traffic. I'm not one of those people, and these final 11 miles for the day convince Christine that she's not, either. The traffic adds stress to the ride that takes the joy right out of it. It's loud and smells bad, and the shoulder has all sorts of road junk in it.

By the time we get to Jefferson City (Jeff City if you're local), we feel more beat up than we did yesterday. We've ridden 67 miles, which is more than I said we would when the day began. The potholes and washed-out sections of the trail took a toll on us, and the unexpected hills and traffic at the end of the day mounted the coup de grâce.

But still, we're delighted to finally have our destination in sight as we roll toward town. To get to Jeff City from the Katy Trail, you need to leave the trail on a spur. While we're not on the trail itself, we are parallel to it on the highway, and we maneuver our way to the route of that spur, following it to a place beneath the bridge that crosses the Missouri. They've constructed a very cool ramp arrangement that allows cyclists and pedestrians to get from the ground down by the river up to the bridge elevation—a square "loop" that spirals up, eventually dropping us off at the bikeway/walkway attached to the bridge, crossing the river but separated from traffic.

All through the day, my biggest fear has been crossing this bridge. The information I could glean online wasn't clear on whether there was a safe way for cyclists to cross or not, making it sound like there was a path separated from traffic, but that this path was sometimes open and sometimes closed. After a long and trying day, this clever elevating square corkscrew and the pathway separated from the highway paint a smile across my face and leave a sweet feeling of relief in my soul.

I can feel Christine brighten behind me as my mood lifts. It's been a trying day, but right now, the world feels splendid, and I love the little slice of goodness that the universe has served up to me.

Life is wonderful.

CHAPTER SIX

JEFFERSON CITY AND THE CLIFF MANOR INN

…as for me, give me comfort first, and style afterwards.
~ **Mark Twain**, *A Connecticut Yankee in King Arthur's Court*

The driveway up to the Cliff Manor Inn is our final little incline of the day, and Christine is unclipping and ready to swing out of the saddle before the bike is stopped all the way. Bone weary, we find the energy to continue our "end-of-day selfie" tradition before heading to the front door where we're greeted by Liz, who shows us around the old mansion and points out the keys to the garage where we can store our bike.

I lock the bike in the garage while Christine is taking her shower, then poke around the beautiful old mansion. As was the case back at the Haysler House in Clinton, there's a decanter of sherry and a few glasses perched invitingly on a sideboard. I fill two glasses and return to our room bearing this welcome treat, greatly appreciated by Christine, whose mood has brightened significantly with the completion of our day, a beautiful room overlooking the Missouri River, a warm and refreshing shower, and now a glass of sweet sherry.

Clean and feeling much more human, we stroll around the area looking for an open restaurant. The neighborhood has the feel of a beautiful old river town, the stately mansions like the one we're staying in perched here on the right bank of the Missouri. While there are restaurants within walking distance none are open, owing possibly to the fact that it's Monday, or possibly to the fact that this is an old downtown district that doesn't see much foot traffic in the evening. So we call a Domino's a few miles away and have pizza delivered. There's a magical culinary fusion that occurs on a pizza crust which, in my experience, makes it a nearly perfect end-of-day feast for the touring cyclist.

We sleep marvelously, surrounded by a beautiful room on the top floor and nestled in one of the most comfortable beds I can remember, waking to a glorious morning. Our habit is to have breakfast as early as we can then get out on the bike before it gets too hot. After the delicious early breakfast that Liz prepares for us, we find ourselves drawn out onto the delightful back porch to enjoy sunshine streaming in and wrapping us in a warm welcome that's hard to walk away from. We decide that since we have less than 50 miles in front of us today, we'll relax on the porch for a while, chat, and nibble on leftover pizza. Which, it turns out, is also a satisfying morning snack for the cyclist looking to crank their training diet up to the next level.

The slowly swirling surface of the Missouri River stretches out beyond the porch. It's easy for my imagination to conjure up an image of Jim coaching Huck Finn as the two of them drift down the river on their raft. Notwithstanding the fact that Jim and Huck drifted down the Mississippi River rather than the Missouri River, the image is palpable here in the heart of Mark Twain country, and it brings a warm smile to my face as I enjoy another piece of leftover pizza.

The clock has rolled past the checkout time of 11:00 by the time Christine and I climb onto our saddles, snap our morning selfie with the Missouri River behind us, and pedal our way back across the river. We coast down the spiral of the uber-cool structure that connects the elevated bridge with the ground below, then begin our trek east along the trail.

CHAPTER SEVEN
JEFFERSON CITY TO HERMANN

There isn't time--so brief is life--for bickerings, apologies, heartburnings, callings to account. There is only time for loving--& but an instant, so to speak, for that.
~**Mark Twain**, *Letter to Clara Spaulding, August 20, 1886*

It's a short ride to the Jeff City trailhead at the Katy Trail along the Katy Trail Spur, where we continue our journey east. Within a mile we're back into the pattern that we enjoyed so much yesterday, with lush hardwood forest rising on our left and farmland spreading out to our right.

After about 13 miles we pass Tebbetts and lean our bike up against a bridge along the trail. The small bridge that crosses the creek here is an ideal place for us to lean the bike as we take a break, complete with a handrail along the top to set our water bottles as we chew a snack, which this morning happens to be the last remaining piece of pizza from our feast last night.

I sip water and savor pizza while Christine swats mosquitos, sips water, swats mosquitos, and crunches a granola bar. And swats mosquitos. Our respite is brief as a result of the little biting vermin, and within a few minutes we're spinning down the trail once again. So long as we keep moving, the loathsome little things can't zero in on her.

The washouts along the trail have gotten worse as we've proceeded east. Today there are places where the trail is gone completely. Several times we choose to get off the trail and ride on Highway 94, which parallels the trail along most of its route. Fortunately, the traffic on the highway is light and extremely courteous.

I'm reminded again how much I enjoy riding on back roads like this, where people are generous and kind as they share the road with cyclists. Of course there is the occasional jerk, but they're by far the exception rather than the rule. If the washouts are going to run me off the trail now and then, I can't think of a better road to enjoy than this one.

For the last several days, I've been flirting along the edges of a dance with a dichotomy as we've made our way through the small towns along the trail, and in Mokane I find myself stepping solidly onto the dance floor with possibly opposing perspectives. It's a dichotomy that might be a tiny reflection of a disconnect happening across America today, and it's a growing gap in understanding who we are and what we're about in this country.

Christine and I are here as journeyers, guests of the fine people who live along the trail. While the trail is an adventure for us, it's home to the folks who live here. As a bicycle tourist, this is not new to me. I'm accustomed to being the odd duck and to adapting myself to the customs and rules of the place I'm traveling through. But I came to the Katy Trail with a slightly different expectation than traveling on the open road, an expectation that might have grown out of my experiences on this and other trails in the past.

Specifically, I seem to be looking for towns along the trail to have embraced the trail as an attraction with which they can build a symbiotic relationship, providing local business with opportunities to cater to users of the trail. This preconceived notion was spawned in my understanding that many small towns across America are losing their young people and their businesses, and that the trail represents an opportunity for these towns to leverage the traffic that travels along it into new business for their towns.

This isn't a notion that I've just made up. I'm remembering two or three stops along the trail back in 2012 where towns had done this. Way back in the 1970s, I took several trips along the early rail trails in Wisconsin, and I hold memories of the touristy feel (that I eschewed at the time) of small Midwest towns along the trail even back then. These memories have worked to build within me an expectation that every town would want to embrace the potential opportunities that a cycling trail and the people who use it, most especially those towns that have suffered the most from the economic flight that many rural towns have experienced.

This notion is out on the dance floor with me alongside my experience of kindness on the backroads of America throughout my life. From bicycling to hunting and fishing to simple backroads exploring, I've always felt heartwarmed by the graciousness of the people I meet and interact with in rural America. Jerks exist and can be found in rural America like anywhere else in the world, but like everywhere else, they're the exception rather than the rule.

This overwhelmingly positive experience swells the unfair expectations I've been developing. Not only am I expecting small towns to see the economic opportunity that the trail represents, I also seem to expect them to be downright Mayberry friendly about it.

This is where my little dance with dichotomy becomes a full-scale romp. It's possible that if I live in a small rural town in America in 2016, I don't want to be importing urban ideas of economic success into my world. If I've seen population and economic decline in my town, I may not even be unhappy about that decline in prosperity. And if I am unhappy about it, I may not see a silly bike trail through town as a solution to that decline. I may want a return to a time I remember in the past, when my town was prosperous and filled with good and happy people making a living in a world that was different from the one I see today.

I can easily imagine feeling that the decline of my community is a result of urban expansion and of the lure of big dollars in the city at the cost of the rural values that I hold dear. If I feel that way, then I'm not about to try and build a symbiotic relationship with a silly rail trail or with the people who use that trail. The trail and the people who use it represent the thing that has hurt my home. The last thing I need is to have more people lured away from town, or to have what I see as unhealthy urban or suburban values infecting my community. The people using the trail should be avoided, even feared, for what they bring and represent.

Of course this is a broad, generalized possibility, and one that may very well be remote or even unlikely. But it's a possibility that I hadn't really considered before. So on those rare occasions when my expectation of kind and gracious small-town shopkeepers is challenged, I'm forced into a bit of intellectual cavorting to understand a perspective that I hadn't considered.

Here in Mokane, my dance with dichotomy has come clearly into focus for me. There's a small general store in town where you can buy groceries, but there's nothing on the trail to let you know it's there. Christine and I really need to fill our water bottles, so we take the quarter-mile side trip down the road with the hope that we'll find someplace to get water. We discover the store, but we don't feel very welcomed. The owner must have bikes come to the store to buy supplies, because there's a big sign in front telling cyclists NOT to lean their bikes on the glass front. And hey, I get that; big plate glass is expensive, and

I wouldn't want bikes leaned against it either. But if I wanted the business of the people riding those bikes, wouldn't I give them an alternative place to lean or park their bikes? Since no alternative is present, I wheel our bike around to the side of the building and lean it there.

Inside, our reception is cool as well. Christine starts up a conversation with the woman behind the counter about grandchildren, which results in a thawing of the chill that we felt when we walked in. I buy a gallon of water and a bag of ice, along with a couple of items from the shelves that will suffice as lunch. There is a table in the store where we sit and enjoy our food and water, and the dance steps that I need to learn begin to take shape for me.

I don't know if this woman is the owner, but I can only suspect that she is. I don't understand her perspective on this small town that is at least the place where she makes her living, and is likely her home as well. I don't know what her experiences with cyclists have been in the past, and I can only hope that she hasn't had a bad experience with a jerk cyclist. All I know for sure is that my perspective has me expecting that she would want to put a sign up along the trail telling cyclists that they should come down to her store and enjoy the nice air conditioning and a cold drink, that she would want to put up a bike rack out front to make it easy for cyclists to park their bike, and that she would want to welcome cyclists who walk through the door, because they represent a nice supplemental revenue stream for her cash register.

By the end of our trip across Missouri, we will have experienced both ends of this spectrum, from heartwarming hospitality to cool rejection, with far more experiences leaning toward hospitable than hostile. Each encounter that feels at all distant from gracious hospitality forces me back onto the dance floor with dichotomy, dancing around, trying to understand a perspective that I didn't expect.

Gathering our water bottles and mounting up, I find myself longing for something that feels like "oh so much more" than just a place to stop.

The next 20 miles repeats the beautiful pattern of hardwood forest rising on our left and rich farmland on our right. The trail approaches the west side of Rhineland along the north side of the highway, crosses the highway before entering town, then crosses back to the north side of the highway east of town. There are supplies available in Rhineland, and if a rider wanted to stop it would make sense to ride along the highway through town instead of on the trail. As it is, we decide that we're close enough to the end of the day to continue east without stopping at Rhineland.

At McKittrick, the trail goes under the highway. We get off the trail just prior to the tunnel and ride south along Highway 19 for a mile into Hermann. We've never been to Hermann, and it's reputed to be a fun little German town along the river, so we've planned to take a day off tomorrow and enjoy the town. We find our way to the Cady Winterset Cottage, where we're greeted by Christine Cady, who'll be our host for the next two days.

Ms. Cady has taken the old carriage house next to her home and converted it into a cozy vintage grotto of memorabilia from the 18th century. Every nook and cranny of the cottage is full of some piece of history or nostalgia, and I imagine a person could spend a day simply exploring this space.

Our showers complete, our gear put away, our tired bodies dressed for walking around town, we head out the door to explore Hermann. The door to our carriage house actually opens onto the alley, which we follow down to Schiller Street, then we turn left toward downtown. It's a quiet walk; few stores are open even as we make our way down to the main drag, which is First Street.

It's early Tuesday evening, and most merchants and restaurants in this town (that appears to rely heavily on tourism) won't begin their week until tomorrow. In small tourist towns, Monday (and in some cases Tuesday) are often their "weekend," so our options for dinner are limited. As we make our way east on First Street, we spot the Hermann Wurst Haus, which appears to be open and toward which we make a beeline. My mouth is watering as we walk in the front door, assailed by the rich and tangy aroma of simmering kraut.

It's 5:50, and although the good folks running the restaurant are getting ready to close down in ten minutes at 6:00, they're kind enough to serve us some outstanding traditional German food, which we relish along with some local wine. We enjoy our meal while the employees go about their closing activities, unlocking the door and thanking us in a friendly and sincere way as we leave.

Strolling back west on First Street, which runs along the river and through town, we notice several couples ambling along, apparently looking for a place to eat supper. One couple sees that we just left the Wurst Haus, and asks if they're open, to which we can only sadly shake our heads and explain that we were their last customers for the day, and that they closed 30 minutes ago.

The guy seems livid. Beyond indignant. He rants for a few minutes about how frustrating it is to drive to this tourist town for a few nights away, and find that most of the town is shuttered because it's not the weekend. As Christine and I walk quietly away, I think about the closed shops in Hermann, and relate it back to the small-town dichotomy I've been dancing with.

While Hermann would still be called a small town, it's one that's embraced tourism and tourists wholeheartedly. I'd go so far as to say that the town's economy is largely *driven* by tourism. And yet, on a September Tuesday evening with quite a few tourists knocking about town, not one of the many restaurants is open.

Which could be either a strong statement of values or purely an economic decision. It could be that merchants in town have simply decided that the town needs a weekend without commerce, and that the weekend is defined as Monday and Tuesday since everyone is busy with tourists on Saturday and Sunday. This is easy for me to understand, based on my own experiences earlier in life.

For two summers, when I was 15 and 16 years old, I lived at Lake of the Ozarks in Missouri. During the second of those summers, I lived on a dock. Literally, a tiny little corner storage room on a covered dock had been emptied out so I could keep a cot in there to sleep. It was a marina, and I worked at the marina six days a week, thirteen hours a day, in exchange for room and board and $25 a week.

It was a pretty ideal job for a teenage boy. An opportunity to spread my wings a bit and stretch my horizons. On my own, accountable to nobody except the old couple who owned the marina and fed me. Of course, working thirteen hours a day and six days a week, there was only so much trouble I could get into. Still, now and again, I'd stumble into a little mischief, or it would stumble into me.

I figure it's fairly difficult to keep teenage boys separated completely from fracas. They'll usually find each other one way or another. We're like magnets during those years, pulling ourselves into tumult we didn't even know was there. Of course, the fact that we're near blind with some rich concoction of powerful hormones coursing through our bodies doesn't reduce that magnetism in any way. Not to mention the apparent inability of the male teenage brain to engage more than about a dozen brain cells at any given time.

Weekends at the marina were crazy busy as the tourists

flooded the lake, churning the water with frenzied devotion to serious recreation and party time. Then Monday would come along, and we'd all take a breath and enjoy the beauty of the place where we lived, now mostly devoid of the crazy tourists. Monday was my day off, my day of rest, my seventh day. And during those days of rest, there was a good bit of time for the sort of deep reflection that we all need at that stage in life when we're discovering who we are and who we want to be.

It's this recollection that I'm pondering as we walk past the closed shops and restaurants, reminding me of what it's like to live in a tourist setting. This is a tourist town, through and through, and Sunday evening is their Friday night, followed by Monday and Tuesday, when they get to have their weekend. Sure it's a bit frustrating to those of us on a different schedule, but we're here as visitors, guests in this quaint tourist town.

The other possibility is that it's purely economics. While it might appear to me that there are quite a few folks strolling the streets in search of place to spend money, it may not actually be enough volume to support the cost of opening the doors. Who am I to make that judgment?

Most likely it's a combination of both things. The folks who live and work here want a weekend, and the extra dollars they'd earn by keeping the doors open on their "weekend" just aren't compelling enough to sacrifice the value they get from a weekend.

We've made our way a block north over to Wharf Street, which runs alongside a park that fronts the river. While everything I've seen of Hermann so far makes me feel like I'm in a fanciful German town, Wharf Street moves me solidly into a 19th-century Missouri river town. The street is only two blocks long but may be my favorite part of town so far, the old buildings reflecting the nature of the business they were constructed to support along the river landing of a bustling and energetic town, which is what it appears Hermann was 150 years ago.

Hermann was established in the mid-19th century by German settlers. My mind conjures up a group of enthusiastic Germans looking to create a slice of their homeland here in the New World, wanting to perpetuate traditional German culture and establish a self-supporting colony built around farming, commerce, and industry. When I read that the town is named after Hermann der Cherusker, a Germanic leader who defeated three Roman legions at the Battle of the Teutoburg Forest in the year 9, I figure that's a pretty apt symbol of the industrious and powerful spirit of the early settlers here.

As I read signs and learn more of the history of the town, my early assumptions about the town are challenged. I'd assumed that the early settlers were attracted to the hilly region because it reminded them of their homeland, and that the grape growing and wine making was an outgrowth of the culture that they brought with them. Which isn't the case at all. What really happened is that the early German settlers were promised fertile farmland by the people who established the town and recruited emigrants to move there, but when they arrived they found heavily timbered rocky hills. So they adapted, observing the abundance of wild grapes, and decided to make wine. Hey, when life gives you grapes, make grape juice. Then let it ferment.

The town held its first Weinfest in the fall of 1848, a tradition that continues today. The quality of the wine in those early years is said to have been mediocre at best, improving dramatically in the mid-1800s thanks to the work of George Husmann, whose father had purchased a Hermann lot while the family was still living in Germany. A self-taught scientist, Husmann studied soil types and crossed wild and cultivated grapes to create hybrids that could survive and thrive in Missouri's hot, humid summers and freezing winters.

Husmann's research saved the vineyards of southern France when they were devastated by phylloxera, a blight spread by aphids. Missouri grape growers shipped 17 carloads of phylloxera-resistant root stock to France. Montpellier in France erected two statues in thanks and commemoration, one depicting a young woman cradling an old woman in her arms, a representation of the New World saving the Old World. This strikes me as yet one more very close tie between our nation and France, ties that we often forget in our recollection of history. Husmann eventually moved from Hermann to California, where he became a founding father of the Napa Valley wine industry.

By the end of the 19th century, Hermann had become one of the largest wine producing regions in the world. Nearly 10% of all U.S. wine on the market in 1904 was from the 11,000 acres of terraced vineyards that covered the hillsides in and around Hermann. Stone Hill Winery—the largest in the area—was the second largest winery in the country, with a vast network of underground cellars that is still among the largest in the world. The famous Apostle Cellar held 12 enormous casks, each carved with the likeness of one of the Apostles. Eight underground cellars at Stone Hill Winery stored a total of 1.25 million gallons of wine.

In 1919, Hermann was introduced to the Great Depression earlier than the rest of the nation when the Volstead Act was passed, creating disaster for a region whose economy was based on making wine. The temperance movement smothered economies across Missouri, bringing the golden era of world-class winemaking to an abrupt and bitter end.

Many here in the region believe this early plunge into the darkness of the Great Depression is what preserved Hermann as the quaint tourist town that it has become. The area was left behind and forgotten as the rest of the nation struggled through the '20s and '30s and '40s, the local German population preferring to stay isolated due to the anti-German prejudice that was prevalent in American culture during the period.

In the mid-60s a renaissance of the winemaking industry began in the region, and along with it came the blossoming of the tourist industry, a patron of which Christine and I are this evening as we wander along the old streets and admire the architecture.

Relaxed and full from a fine dinner, we find our way back up our alley and to the front door of the lovingly decorated Cady Winterset Cottage. We enjoy a quiet and peaceful evening sitting on the front porch, finishing the bottle of local wine that we began back at the Wurst Haus, before retiring to our grotto in the converted carriage house.

CHAPTER EIGHT

HERMANN AND THE CARRIAGE HOUSE INN

When you fish for love, bait with your heart, not your brain.
~ **Mark Twain**, *From His Notebook, 1898*

Wednesday morning finds us sitting at the little table outside our front door at the Cady Winterset Cottage, also known as the Carriage House Bed & Breakfast, enjoying the quiet of the alley that our carriage house fronts. Well, mostly quiet, that is. A couple of doors down and across the alley there appears to be some fun and celebration going on. Last night as we were walking home we heard similar gaiety and wondered if there was a wedding party lodging at the Captain Wohlt Inn, but we're surprised to hear them up so early this morning and enjoying themselves.

It's not long before bicycles start to trickle past us down the alley, and it becomes clear to us that the boisterous sounds are the result of breakfast shared among a collection of cyclists, and they're percolating down the alley toward the bridge now, headed for a day on the Katy Trail.

Curiosity gets the best of me and I wander over to learn about the group. I chat with Bubba, who's the ringleader. He operates Bubba's Pampered Pedalers and does a Katy Trail trip about every year. Bubba's is one of a growing number of companies who've emerged to cater to touring cyclists who'd like someone else to do the planning and schlep the gear. I ask Bubba what they did about supper since no place was open, and he said that they typically manage eating arrangements for the group, staying at places who'll also bring food in or let them prepare it.

Back on our front porch, I ask Christine about this, wondering how she'd feel as part of a larger group like that. We both agree that while there are some great advantages to having someone else take care of all those details, it also means that we'd miss out on the adventure of discovering things for ourselves along the way.

Ms. Cady has a morning table fit for royalty set for us as we wander over to her porch at our agreed 9:00 breakfast time. The food is not only delicious, but it's prepared and presented as if we were in a five-star restaurant. Our agreed breakfast time this morning is a little later than usual, but perfect for our day of wandering around and enjoying this historic *stadt*.

We meander up and down every street that looks even slightly interesting, enjoying the beautifully preserved architecture and feeling encouraged by the increase in "Open" signs we're seeing in windows. A sweet shop called Sugar Momma's is packed with sugary delights and touristy baubles, and being the good tourists that we are, we feel compelled to partake in a few of the more decadent consumable indulgences, though we talk each other out of buying any trinkets that would represent extra weight in our panniers.

Looking east, we see a beautiful old church and trudge up the steep hill that brings us to Saint George Catholic Church, a gorgeous old structure initially completed in 1850. After a few pictures, we glance across the tops of the hills around us from this high point and see another old church on the next hill over toward the river.

Down one steep hill and up another we go, ending up at

Saint Paul United Church of Christ. Built about the same time
as Saint George, these two structures are visible for miles and
lend a strong pastoral feel to the town. The view out across the
river from Saint Paul's could easily be a view somewhere in the
Rhine valley, and we dawdle for quite a while taking pictures
and enjoying the quiet.

The water below and serenity around me remind me again
of those magical summers of my teenage years, living in an
environment supported by tourism, and I'm happy that we've
now arrived at Wednesday, the first day of the work week in this
tourist town, when the shops are generally going to be open.

We've been keeping our eyes open all day for a coffee shop,
and while there's no Starbucks, the map shows a coffee shop on
the east side of town called Espresso Laine. Our trip across town
from the east side (where Saint Paul church is) to the west side
(where the coffee shop is) can be measured in steps rather than
miles—really you can see from one side of town to the other,
though you can't read the signs. Arriving at Espresso Laine, we
spend a wonderful half hour sitting on their porch and drinking some excellent coffee. Taking a look at their hours, I'm im-
pressed that they're open seven days a week. I suppose a local
coffee shop, frequented by local folks, would get the support
they need to be open every day.

After coffee we enjoy a tour at the Hermannhof Vineyards,
where we're allowed to wander the old cellar. While we're dis-
ciplined enough not to purchase any heavy trinkets that we'd
have to carry, we do manage to spend a little money for some
wine to enjoy later in the day.

We spend the rest of the day relaxing, strolling, and reading,
finishing with an early supper. Yesterday evening one of the
restaurants that looked like an interesting place to eat but was
closed was named Simon's on the Waterfront. We decide to give
that a try tonight, arriving at the front door to discover a short
hallway, at the end of which is a door on the right that takes us

into the bar, and another on the left leading to the restaurant. We look at each other, both tilting our head toward the bar side, and head that way.

Opening the door, we're smothered in a thick roil of cigarette smoke, and we see patrons scattered around the room with drifts of smoke rising from cigarettes resting in ashtrays or held in fingertips. We turn and retreat into the restaurant, pleased that it appears to be free of smoke. Before ordering, we confirm with the server that smoking isn't allowed here on the restaurant side.

Cigarette smoking is one of those cultural evolutions that speaks broadly to our adaptability as social creatures. Christine and I both grew up in the 50s and 60s, when it was not only socially acceptable to smoke, but in many circles, almost socially expected. Cars were filled with smoke and offices were swamped in it, and restaurants provided ashtrays on every table. I remember when restaurants began to offer a "no smoking" section, and the grumbles from smokers that this notion evoked. In the 80s, when the office that I worked in made the decision to limit smokers to smoking in their own offices but not in the common areas of the office, they felt like they were being mistreated. Then when we took the absurd step of banning smoking inside altogether, they were outraged.

Walking into Simon's bar as it swims in cigarette smoke reminds me of those days, and it makes me realize that everything about life back in those days was bathed in the odor of cigarettes. We didn't even notice it. It was just part of life, part of what we adapted to. Today, living in the world we do, where (at least in most states) it's no longer socially acceptable to smoke where others will need to participate with you whether they want to or not, we're shocked at the overwhelming smell of a bar that allows smoking.

Not to pick on Simon's. I'm sure that the laws in Missouri allow smoking in bars. In fact, the laws here might even allow restaurants to choose whether to be smoke-free or not. And is this a bad thing? Shouldn't I be allowed to choose whether or not to allow smoking in my establishment? Shouldn't the market be able to decide whether or not this is a good idea?

Prior to the 80s, that was our perspective, and it was a rare establishment indeed that would infringe on the rights of the patron who wanted to smoke. The rest of society adapted to the consequence of that freedom of choice. My closet reeked of the smell of stale cigarette smoke, and there was nothing I could do about it. The lungs of my children were treated to secondhand smoke, just as my lungs were when I was growing up.

One man's freedom is another man's chain. Culture in most of our country has evolved now to the place where we've accepted that the freedom to live free of cigarette smoke is more important than the freedom to smoke, though it was painful to get there. Here in Hermann, Missouri, those lines of liberty are drawn a bit differently still. At Simon's they've chosen to let the marketplace make those decisions for them. The marketplace is a living and changing thing, and while it says one thing today, tomorrow could bring a new and different decision.

We sleep deeply then enjoy another fabulous breakfast the next morning, laid out with love and care by Ms. Cady. Our morning selfie reflects two happy cyclists beginning another beautiful day on the Katy Trail.

NOTE: As of the writing of this book, only months after our wonderful day in Hermann, it appears that Simon's On the Waterfront is no longer in business, or at least that's what Google tells me. We'll never know how much the clouds of cigarette smoke contributed to their demise, as the marketplace is both fickle and secretive, allowing the observer to draw their own conclusions about the decisions it makes.

CHAPTER NINE
HERMANN TO AUGUSTA

The holy passion of Friendship is of so sweet and steady and loyal and enduring a nature that it will last through a whole lifetime, if not asked to lend money.

~**Mark Twain**, *Pudd'nhead Wilson's Calendar*

Our ride across the bridge over the Missouri River this morning is much more pleasant than the one two days ago when we entered Hermann. We're both refreshed and happy, bellies full of a delightful breakfast, ready for our adventure to continue. We ride the mile or two up to McKittrick, where we rejoin the Katy Trail to continue east.

We'll ride today with my dear friend Rick, whom we connect with at Joey's Birdhouse bed and breakfast in McKittrick where he spent the night last night. We meet Joey, chat for a while on the front porch, then mount up and head east along the trail.

Rick and I have been friends for over 50 years, starting when we were neighbors growing up. This is the same Rick that I talk about in *Pilgrim Spokes*, the one with whom I rode a portion of the trail back in 2012 when I was crossing the country. We'll ride some of the same trail together today as well as some new territory, as we traverse the next 35 miles or so to Augusta.

We live in a culture of constant change. We go off to college or work, and often leave behind the friends we grew up with. We leave behind college friends when we go off to a career. Most of us change jobs a few times, each time leaving behind one set of coworkers and gaining a new set. Many times those job changes involve a relocation, where we leave behind our old friends and start over in a new place, building a whole new set of friends.

Mentors within our society talk about the value of building a good career, of making something of yourself in the world. There's talk of the importance of friends, but that talk is usually within the context that we need to make friends wherever we are, and that those friends are an important part of our life.

Without a doubt, all this advice and wisdom is true and important. But rarely do we recognize the real value of friendships that span a lifetime. When we're young, we can't fathom that this is a big deal, as we're moving through the adventure of living, greeting life where it meets us, building as we go with the new tools and gifts and people that we meet.

I think it's only when we reach the wise side of 60, as I have, that the real value of these lifelong friendships becomes apparent. It's possible that I was taught this when I was younger, and that I simply didn't pay attention. Maybe I heard it back in those wonderful days when I knew everything, before I entered this dark time of life when there are things I don't know. Back before I learned that I'm not invincible, before I learned that listening is more important than speaking. All the more reason, I think, that we as parents and grandparents need to teach this lesson to those who depend on us for real wisdom, those who don't yet know that they need this wisdom.

This revelation doesn't smack me in the face this morning, but it creeps along the edges of my thoughts as we pedal along, making small talk occasionally. Rich and I share history that goes back half a century. We haven't stayed in close touch over the years, but we were close friends before college, knew each other in college and after college, and have gotten together occasionally over the years. Our small talk reveals just how far back our history goes, and just how much we know about each other.

It feels good to have someone know so much about me. Someone with whom I share such a long history.

At about 16 miles we roll through the community of Treloar, where the trail guide says we can find water. Christine and I are skeptical after our experiences of the past few days, and our skepticism turns out to be well founded. We pedal around looking for even a spigot, as Rick's water bottles are empty, but we find nothing at all. If there are either water or supplies in Treloar, we're not smart enough to find them.

Still, our ride today is a wonderful mix of all that's delightful about the Katy Trail. We ramble through deep woods, then roam across open farmland. Several sections of the trail wind along beside the river as it rolls its way toward the Mississippi.

In the town of Marthasville, we hit the lunchtime jackpot at a place called Philly's Pizza. If there's one place for a cyclist not to miss from one end of the Katy Trail to the other, it's this eatery in Marthasville. It should come as no surprise to us that it's as busy as it is, since both the food and the service are great, and it makes me wonder if some of the other small towns that we've ridden through might also have been able to support a place like this.

We're the only cyclists in the place, though clearly we're not the first. The walls are meant for writing on here and are covered with everything from signatures to notes left for other cyclists to long descriptions of the ride. There's nothing about this place that indicates that it is here for cyclists, or that they particularly cater to cyclists, but it's clear that their arms are open to cyclists. We feel welcome.

At first glance it's easy to oversimplify this and say that this just proves that all you have to do is open a place up along the trail and welcome cyclists, and you'll have a success. But the issue deserves a deeper look.

For starters, Marthasville has a reported population of about 1000. A small town for sure, but still not nearly as small as many of the communities and towns we've ridden through. Mokane, where we were disappointed in the surly reception we got from the little general store, has a reported population of 10. (That's right, ten people—I didn't leave off a zero.) Rocheport was trying hard to be a welcome place for cyclists, and a hub for activity along the trail, and they have a reported population of about 250. Hartsburg, population just over 100, was also trying to be welcoming to cyclists, but they clearly needed the weekend volume of riders to justify "Open" signs in the windows.

Here we are, prosperous folks from a thriving state growing by 100,000 people a year, and it's taken a few days for a different reality to settle in on me. (According to the U.S. Census Bureau, Colorado's population reached 5,456,574 as of July 1, 2015, up from 5,355,588 the same day a year earlier.) The picture in rural America, as exemplified along the Katy Trail here, is quite different. Many small towns have been shriveling for decades, as young folks seek jobs in the city and big box stores lure the remaining population away from the few small-town merchants who remain to try and scrape out a living.

From a pure dollars and cents perspective, the practice of welcoming cyclists would be a good idea for any merchant who's already running a business along the trail. It's unlikely that a person could open a business just to target cyclists, but if the doors are already open, then even if it's only one extra customer a day, it's still one extra customer a day. And within the cycling community the word does, indeed, get out. Cyclists will frequent the places recommended by others in their tribe.

As with everything, the simple answer is rarely the whole truth.

Here in Marthasville the population appears to be large enough to support a small place like Philly's, and embracing the traffic along the Katy Trail. The three of us enjoy an excellent meal and good conversation, grateful for a fun place to stop and eat along the trail.

Our destination today is Augusta, and we've been told to expect trail repair in the final miles approaching town. There are a couple of signs indicating that this is true, so when we're still a few miles out of town we get off the trail and continue our ride along Augusta Bottom Road. It's a flat road with no traffic, and we enjoy the delightful pavement beneath our tires.

Approaching Augusta, the road takes a steep upward tilt for a short distance, followed by a nice ride along a ridge above town. The road here is called High Street, and it's easy to understand why, as we have beautiful views into the valleys around us. We pass a few wineries before dropping sharply into and through town, noticing the Ashley's Rose Restaurant as we pass, thinking this might be a fun place to come back to for supper.

Thunderheads have gathered around us, and we're thankful to have arrived at the Red Brick Inn before the rain begins. It's been a delightful day, and while we're tired, we're happy. Our riding for the day ends with smiles all around. I'm swathed in a feeling of goodness as I roll our bike into the shed beneath the porch and make my way inside to join Christine and Rick.

CHAPTER TEN

AUGUSTA AND THE RED BRICK INN

When I was younger, I could remember anything, whether it had happened or not; but my faculties are decaying now and soon I shall be so I cannot remember any but the things that never happened.
~**Mark Twain**, *Autobiography*

O ne hour and a hot shower later, we're ready for supper. Apparently the Silly Goose is the place to go for supper, but it's early still, and we don't want to wait until they open at 5:00. Instead, we walk back to the Ashley's Rose Restaurant, which appears to be in the process of opening for the evening.

Ashley's Rose is an eclectic place, with airplane relics everywhere, including what appears to be the entire frame of an old open-cockpit Piper Cub hanging from the ceiling. It's a fun place to sit and chat, and while we're happy to have a fun place to eat supper, we wish we would have waited for the Silly Goose to open, based on the great things people have to say about it.

Thunderstorms roil all around us as we walk out of Ashley's Rose, the sky descending with a downpour. We wait for a break in the deluge and gallop through wet streets back down the hill to the Red Brick Inn, where our hosts Chuck and Esther have wine sitting out on the kitchen counter to welcome us back home. Turns out they have a happy hour every day at 5:00 for their guests. I'm not sure if this is common practice at bed and breakfast establishments here in this area surrounded by wineries, but it's a great idea that we're delighted to take advantage of and enjoy.

The Red Brick Inn is a new establishment here in Augusta. Chuck and Esther moved from their home in Saint Louis out here to Augusta about a year ago and bought this place. They spent the winter getting it fixed up, and they opened this past May. It's a wonderful 1860s Federalist-style home that they've done an excellent job of turning into a welcoming bed and breakfast.

Christine and I take our wine out onto the big gazebo off the back deck where Rick is waiting for us and enjoy a beautiful evening unfolding in the Missouri hills. The rain has stopped for the time being, leaving behind air that's dense and damp, soaking our sinuses and lungs with welcome moisture. Christine and I take our daily selfie here on the deck today, happy and smiling with beautiful Missouri woodland in the background.

It's interesting to me that I view humidity as such a positive thing these days. Growing up in the Midwest, humidity was uncomfortable, something that made summers sticky and winters miserable. Dry air was a thing to be pursued and enjoyed. After living in the arid high plains of eastern Colorado for the past 20 years, I've learned to appreciate humidity when I'm around it.

Sitting under the gazebo, enjoying the heavy air of late afternoon and the sounds of birds in the trees around us, I hear what sounds like a pileated woodpecker not far away. I grab my iPhone and open my Merlin Bird ID app (oh the wonders of modern technology), and immediately bring up the pileated woodpecker, clicking on the option to play the sounds that a pileated makes. While my objective is to validate that the sound I'm hearing in the woods close by is, indeed, a pileated, we're rewarded within seconds by the real woodpecker flying straight out of the woods and making itself comfortable in a nearby tree, waiting for this new bird to sing again. Not wanting to create too much confusion in the animal world, I turn off the app, delighted by this cool use of technology to help us see a shy and spectacular bird that we might otherwise have missed.

While I gloat, Christine swats the hoard of mosquitos that have discovered her sweet flesh, before deciding that inside and away from bugs is the place to be right now. Rick and I pack up and follow her in, finishing our glass of wine inside. Rick suggests that we go downtown where they're having some sort of festival, but Christine isn't crazy about the notion of offering up any more blood to the mosquitos today, so Rick and I head downtown on our own.

The festival, it turns out, is their annual Augusta Harvest Festival, this year titled "Swingin' in the Vines." They hope to raise enough money to refurbish their old VFW post, called Harmony Hall, by selling bricks for $100 each, as well as various other fundraising activities.

It's a perfect way to spend a summer evening with an old friend, sitting on a picnic table, drinking an iced tea, watching people around me who are all good friends and neighbors, coming together to kick off a weekend of "raising." As I watch the good-natured elbow rubbin', gossip, and occasional flirting around me, I think about the word "raising" and how some form of its meaning has been rattling around in my brain on this ride.

In this case, the folks who live here are raising funds to do something good together in their town. The Amish will have a barn raising where everyone comes together to stand up a barn in a day for a neighbor. Rick and I both raised our families with the help of friends and extended family around us. All these things involve people coming together to build their community, to improve their village, to strengthen their tribe.

A small group of friends is up in the gazebo playing music,

chatting occasionally with friends that wander by and raising a glass of beer in their direction. Fifty yards away from us a flock of half a dozen young girls has gathered around a picnic table, laughing just a little too loudly and being slightly too animated as they watch the tiny pack of boys out of the corner of their eye. The boys, in turn, hit each other playfully and strut about like roosters, checking the flock of girls every minute or so to be sure they're still being watched.

Rick and I are clearly outsiders here, but folks don't seem to mind—they walk up and talk to us more than once as we carry on our conversation and observation. Our "outsider" status makes things only slightly awkward since the people who walk up to us are genuinely friendly, not making it feel like forced conversation.

I'm not a naturally gregarious person; in fact, I've often been accused of having somewhat hermit-ish tendencies. While I can be social when it's called for, I tend to avoid those situations, preferring a quiet discussion with a friend rather than mingling with strangers. Rick is no more social than I am. In fact, if there were a scale for this sort of thing, where "ten" was a social butterfly and "one" was a hermit, I'm fairly sure I'd rank below a "five." Whatever my ranking might be, it would be higher than Rick's. In fact, I suspect that the folks at Myers-Briggs might have been tempted to come up with a fifth character in their Myers-Briggs Type Indicator scale when Rick took the test—an exclamation point behind the "I" for introvert. The fact that folks come up and talk to us a few times speaks volumes about the friendliness of the crowd, even if it makes Rick and me a little uncomfortable.

Our conversation dances around those subjects that most 60-something folks probably talk about: failing memories and changes in our attitudes as we've gotten older. And of course, it's impossible for two men in their 60s to have a conversation and not complain about the fact that we have to pee so much more often than we did when we were young and robust.

I like having these conversations. It makes me feel more normal, like things will be okay. It's hard to feel your brain changing, forgetting things more than you once did, and not feel worried. I feel great about the life I've had and the life I'm having, and I have absolutely zero fear about walking out of this life. But Alzheimer's is not the path I want to take. Every time I forget something that I don't think I should have forgotten, I worry. But talking to other folks my age who have similar experiences helps me feel like it'll be okay.

"I asked my doctor about it," I say to Rick. "He said not to worry too much about it. Says it's common for memory to change as we age. He gave me this little verbal quiz as a high-level screen, and he said that really, he didn't see any need to test any further."

Rick is staring off into the distance. I learned a long time ago that Rick does this, and while it might appear that he's not paying attention, he is. I sit for a few seconds, then I add, "I hope he's right."

"What sorts of questions were on the quiz?" Rick asks.

"I can't remember." I don't say it to be funny, but in the context, it makes us both laugh heartily.

Our conversation drifts around a bit, working its way into the difference we've both noticed in our level of tolerance over the years, learning to take things as they come. Rick is unusually spirited about the subject.

"Like the first kid you have, and how everything has to be just exactly right, and they have to behave just exactly right, or you're sure they won't turn out right," he says.

"Right, then by the time the third one rolls around you've figured out that they're gonna turn out just fine, and that you don't need to be in control of every single thing that happens in their life."

Rick laughs as he replies, "Or in my case by the time the fifth one rolls around you figure out that too much meddling is more likely to do harm than good!"

"You know," I say, "I always thought that folks get less tolerant and more set in their ways as they get older. I don't feel like that's happening to me. In fact, sometimes I feel the opposite, like I'm becoming far more tolerant and accepting of change than I was when I was younger."

"I suppose it depends on what kind of change you're talking about. I think I'm pretty set in my daily routine, but I do think I'm more accepting of changes in the world around me."

"Yeah, I agree. I like the things and habits of my life; depending on them gives me security. But when it comes to a willingness to see the perspective and point of view of other people, I find myself far more open and adaptable than I was earlier in life. You know what I mean? And it's not what I expected."

"We always hear about how we close our minds as we get older, and I agree with you, I don't see it happening with me."

"Or maybe it is, and we've just deluded ourselves into thinking that our minds are staying open when really they're closed so tightly that we can't even see that they're closed!"

Rick smiles, then adds, "Either way, I suppose the key is just staying open to new ideas, and keeping a curious mind."

I take another sip of iced tea, wondering if it really is that simple—just keeping a curious mind. "If it is, indeed, so simple, then why do so many of us get so intransigent as we age? We've lived a lot and seen a lot, and learned that there's nearly always more than one right answer. Wisdom *should* bring mental suppleness and an ability to see and understand subtlety, so why do so many older folks fail to display those characteristics?"

"Well, are you sure they don't? Maybe you're working off a false stereotype. Maybe most older folks are, like us, more able to see things from different perspectives."

"That makes all the sense in the world to me; I'm gonna operate under that assumption for a while."

A middle-aged woman walks up to us, offering a most outstanding brick for the bargain price of $100. While we pass on this particular wonderful deal, we do walk over to the tent by the gazebo where the music is being played. Here in the shade of the canvas, tables are piled with tee shirts and other festival memorabilia for sale, as well as some great homemade cookies and cakes.

Rick's wife, Martha, has convinced him recently that he needs to wear tee shirts that are size L instead of XL. "I've always liked XL tee shirts, because I like the way they hang on me—nice and loose. But she says that the L size fits me better and looks better."

"Maybe you've lost some weight lately?" I ask.

"No, she just says it looks better. Less sloppy, I guess."

I watch as Rick looks through the tee shirt piles. They're very nicely designed tee shirts, and I consider buying one myself; it is a good cause after all. But in the end, good sense wins out; the last thing I need is another tee shirt, especially if it means packing it out on the bicycle. Rick continues checking out all the tee shirts, apparently frustrated with something.

"Whatayadoin' Rick, can't find exactly the right color? They're all the same, you know."

He chuckles. "They don't have my size, all they have is L."

"Uh, I thought you said you wore size L now."

He stops and looks at me a minute with an expression that I'm very familiar with, one that says, "Oh, right … " Then, with a laugh and a shake of the head, picks up a tee shirt, size L, and pays for it.

Walking up the street toward the Red Brick Inn, I comment that it's a really cool design on the tee shirt, to which Rick replies, "Yeah, it is. I suppose I'll never wear it."

"I know that feeling. Already too many tee shirts in the tee shirt drawer, right?"

"No, that's not it. I don't like wearing tee shirts with cool designs, because then strangers are more likely to notice it, and start a conversation by asking about it."

Check out your Webster's. Look up the word "introvert." You'll see Rick's name and picture there.

CHAPTER ELEVEN

AUGUSTA TO ALTON

Pretty soon it darkened up, and begun to thunder and lighten; so the birds was right about it. Directly it begun to rain, and it rained like all fury, too, and I never see the wind blow so. It was one of these regular summer storms. It would get so dark that it looked all blue-black outside, and lovely; and the rain would thrash along by so thick that the trees off a little ways looked dim and spider-webby; and here would come a blast of wind that would bend the trees down and turn up the pale underside of the leaves; and then a perfect ripper of a gust would follow along and set the branches to tossing their arms as if they was just wild; and next, when it was just about the bluest and blackest—FST!

~**Mark Twain**, *The Adventures of Huckleberry Finn*

The weather forecast has been calling for rain early today, then a break in the rain about 10:00. As a result, we've opted for a breakfast later than usual to accommodate a start about 9:30 or 10:00. Although we've got almost 60 miles planned for the day, including a ferry ride across the Mississippi, it'd be nice to avoid a soaking downpour if we can.

At breakfast, we meet Chuck and Carol, who live in a small town in southern Indiana and are here riding the trail, not for the first time. It seems that riding the Katy Trail is an annual thing for them, as it's an easy drive to get here, and they can design a ride of two or three days with stays at nice bed and breakfasts each night. They're not the first people we've met along the trail who do something like this, and I wonder what percentage of trail users live close by in the Midwest and make repeated forays out here to vacation. It's a great idea, and gets me wondering how much success bed and breakfasts might have if they formed loose connections with one another and offered packages to riders that they could advertise regionally. Not really organized tours, as the participants would need to figure out the logistics and deal with getting there, but the package would include lodging, maybe meals, could even include a shuttle if that was desired.

Which brings me back to the thoughts I've been chewing on for these last few days about merchants along the trail recognizing, or in a few cases seemingly not recognizing, the business opportunity that the trail might represent for them. It's not that I'd like to see the Katy Trail turned into a theme park; quite the opposite. I think the Katy Trail is a beautiful treasure, and I'd like to see us (as a society) build more like it. However, I'm also someone who believes in the power of the marketplace, and finding ways for the people who live along the trail to reap additional economic benefit from the trail could go a long way toward increasing trail use while adding convenience for the trail user. Eventually, this might also make the concept more viable for the future rail-trail efforts and dreams that are out there.

Not to mention the more obvious benefit of boosting the local economy for some of the small towns along the trail. Observing the *raising* activities yesterday evening of the good people here in Augusta, I have to believe that even the desire and the attempt to leverage the economic contribution of traffic along the trail might have a positive community impact.

Synergy.

Rick has packed his bike into his car and will head back home from here. We bid our farewells, then Christine and I climb onto our saddles and head to the trailhead, where we turn east and continue our journey. The rain has stopped, though the trail is still generously garnished with standing puddles of water. Fenders would be mighty nice here, a common oversight for those of us who live in Colorado. Although the rack and panniers do a reasonable job of preventing too much rooster-tailing from the back tire, the front tire is blasting my feet and legs with a steady stream of mud from the puddles that are hard to avoid.

About six miles into the ride, the rain starts up again. Beginning as a light drizzle, it intensifies to a downpour within 20 minutes. Before long it's a torrential rain so heavy it pulls leaves off trees, big green wads carried through the river of water falling from the dark sky above us. Rain so thick and heavy it obscures my visibility beyond a few yards, causing me to slow further. Thunder explodes every few seconds, often close enough that it's only a second or two behind the burst of lightning that created the explosion. I'd dearly love to stop and seek some shelter, but all that's around me are trees and trail.

This is not a fun moment. We joke a bit as we ride, or at least we try to joke. It's interesting how moments like this can bring a couple closer. Not that I'd choose this particular moment, or choose the misery we're feeling, but it's clear we're feeling it side by side, in a manner of speaking. We bond tightly as these miles pass, knowing that we're united in our misery, and we'll find a way through it together.

Shared adventures form an important cement for a relationship. The adventure unfolds, stirring moments of delight together with moments of misery, forming a glue that defines the relationship and binds it together. It can be a volatile mixture, and as with any volatile mixture I'm sure there are times when there's more blowup than binding. This morning, with me and Christine, the strengthening connection feels good, a powerful occasion of *kinship*.

There's a covered bench by the Weldon Spring trailhead, where we stop to try and get some protection from the lightning. We sit together on the bench, and I wrap my arm around Christine as she pulls herself deeply into my arms. I move immediately from misery to bliss as we share warmth and comfort, somewhat safe beneath a tiny covering, rain pummeling the ground around our feet while wind, lightning, and thunder rage through the woods above us.

As the rain slows a bit, I take our daily selfie to send to the kids. They turn the image into a meme later, one where Christine is saying something akin to "and this is Neil's idea of fun … "

Our drenched clothes invite a chill to settle on us before long. We can't get any more wet that we are, and since the lightning has moved past us, we decide to climb back on the bike to generate some heat by pedaling our way further down the trail. We've got the bulk of the day's miles in front of us still, and there's a good deal of uncertainty in those miles. The rain has turned the trail into a muddy mess, and we're wondering what it will be like beyond Saint Charles. Will the ferry across the Mississippi still run when it's raining with thunderstorms in the area?

The clouds thin slightly as we approach Saint Charles. The light rain occasionally dissolves into something more like a palpable mist than actual raindrops, then it finds another second wind and spits light drops at us for a while. On a day with different weather, we might be thinking about exploring the old river town, but today we're only looking for a warm and dry place to take a break. Any place at all where there's more warmth and less wet than we're feeling out here in the saddle.

When I rode across this section of trail back in 2012, they were in the process of renovating the riverfront area. At that time, I either got off the trail to ride through town or the trail took me through town, I can't recall which. But I recall riding on streets close to the river, and I remember stopping at a quirky place that was a combination of café and bike shop. I remember standing with my bike outside the store on a warm September day, eating a muffin, chatting with some other cyclists who were riding on the trail.

Christine notices a sign for the Bike Stop Café on our left, and I make a U-turn and guide us back to the place. Pulling up to the front door, I glance around at the place, and I am sure this isn't the same storefront that I stood in front of back in 2012, eating a muffin. But the concept seems the same.

Squishing my way through the front door, I see that Christine has found us a table to sit at and is peeling wet gear off. She's smiling, feeling wonderful to have a warm and dry place to take a break. There's another couple at a table who appear to be cyclists but who are bone dry. We exchange a few words with them, discovering that they're hanging out here waiting to see if the rain stops before they make their way down the trail. They're starting their ride across the Katy here in Saint Charles, headed west, and if it rains all day, they'll change their plans and start their ride tomorrow.

Christine grabs my hand and guides us over to the barista at the coffee counter, where she orders a latte. It seems that even the act of ordering the latte brings her happiness, and I have to admit that the hot black coffee that the barista hands to me is more than just hot liquid—it's an icon of warmth that I wrap my hands around as we make our way back to our table.

Sitting down, I peer around the shop and feel fairly certain that this must be the same place I stopped back in 2012, though my memory of the place where I stopped is a little different from this. But then, my memory isn't all that great. We notice a register for bikers to sign, and we thumb our way back to 2012 but don't see my name. But then, I'm not a big one for signing registers, either.

Jodi is the name of the woman who serves us coffee, and she tells us that the trail is closed east of here because of the torrential rains that have dumped on them all summer. We tell her about the frequent washouts we've been dealing with along the trail, and she confirms that yes, the historic rain that Missouri has experienced this year has dealt a hard blow to the condition of the trail and discouraged a lot of folks from riding on it.

It turns out that Jodi, along with her husband Tony, runs the Bike Stop Café. They opened it back in 2010, and she confirms that in 2012 there was a good deal of riverfront restoration going on, and that they were in a different location. (This clears up for me why I wasn't sure if I'd stopped here back in 2012.) Talking with Jodi, I'm heartened by the fact that they've been able to make a success out of a business catering to cyclists along the trail. While cycling customers make up only a part of the revenue stream in their business model, it's a rather significant part. They also organize river activities and operate a shuttle service.

Christine perks up at the mention of a shuttle service. "So you have a van that you shuttle riders and their bikes in?" she asks.

"We do," Jodi responds. "In fact, Tony has the van out right now picking up some stranded riders."

Christine looks at me with bright hopefulness in her eyes, then turns back to Jodi and asks, "And can the van fit a tandem in it?"

"Oh yeah, we take tandems all the time."

We're about two cups of hot coffee into our task of warming up, along with a cup of excellent soup. It's clear to me that Christine has no desire to relinquish the warmth she's finding here, and frankly I'm not crazy about the idea either. This newly discovered information about a warm shuttle van that could take us past our last 20 miles for the day have added a new option to our conversation, and Christine is warming rapidly to a new possibility to stay dry and safe. When Jodi tells us that she just heard that Highway 67 is closed on this side of the river because of flooding, we're both convinced that a shuttle across the river is the prudent course to take.

CHAPTER TWELVE
ALTON AND THE BEALL MANSION

After all these years, I see that I was mistaken about Eve in the beginning;
it is better to live outside the Garden with her than inside it without her.
~ **Mark Twain**, *Adam's Diary*

When I rode through Alton in 2012 while crossing America, I stopped at the Beall Mansion in Alton, Illinois. I stayed in the Butler's Quarters on the top floor, and I loved the room. Christine and I had been communicating at the time, rekindling our relationship from college, and were planning to connect on the east coast when I finished the ride in Annapolis, which wasn't far from where she lived. Here in Alton, in my room at the Beall, I'd called her on the phone to let her know I was still on schedule. The romantic in me thought it would be fun for us to stay together in that same room at the conclusion of this ride.

Jim checks us in and we lock the bike in the garage, then he walks us around the beautiful old mansion for a tour. It's much the same tour I got four years ago when I stayed here, and I realize as I listen that Jim must've given this tour hundreds of times. His love of this old place is clear in the way he talks about it, even though he could probably do this tour in his sleep.

The love that proprietors have for their old bed and breakfasts has been a constant theme on our journey this past week.
It shined the brightest on our first night of the tour with Roger
back in the Haysler House and his detailed descriptions of the
quarter-sawn oak flooring or some other minute detail of the
old mansion, and I see it again shining as brightly in Jim as he
lovingly describes the history and restoration of the old mansion for which he is steward.

The rain has stopped, so we do some Google mapping to
find a restaurant nearby. We decide on a place that's only a mile
or so away and figure we'll take in the neighborhood as part of
an evening walk to supper. I recall my early-morning departure
from the Beall four years ago, riding a block or two east past
beautiful old mansions, then descending to the river. On our
drive up to the Beall in the shuttle today we approached from
the east along Twelfth Street as well, admiring those beautiful
old homes.

Our walk to supper takes us west this time, away from the
mansions, and the neighborhood around us evolves as we walk,
soon reminding both of us of the working-class neighborhoods
we grew up in. Five young men gather around an old Ford pickup truck, leaning on the truck, an open 12-pack of Budweiser
resting on the tailgate and half consumed while they chat and
laugh. They look our way as we pass, and I give them a little
nod and slight smile, receiving the same in return.

A compact neighborhood grocery rests up against the aging
sidewalk a block further down the street. A diminutive elderly
lady makes her way to her car parked on the curb in front of
the grocery, accompanied by a young grocery boy carrying her
two bags of groceries. After placing the groceries in her trunk,
he opens her car door and holds it patiently while she eases her
way behind the wheel after deliberately placing what is probably a tip into his palm.

The scene caps off the nostalgic fog that we've both felt over the past couple of blocks as the neighborhood has such a similar feel to those we both grew up in. Christine reaches for my hand, and we walk hand in hand the rest of the way to supper.

We're one of only a few customers at the Bluff City Grill, enjoying supper while reliving our last several days of riding in shared memories. The rain begins to spit off and on outside, and we bask in a warm sense of accomplishment after our traverse of the famous Katy Trail. While most folks think of Saint Charles as the eastern terminus of the trail, and would be having their supper to celebrate the ride culmination there, I like that we decided to make our way to Alton. Saint Charles felt like a larger touristy town, and although I'm sure the population of Alton isn't small, here along the river it feels like the small rural towns we've been riding through.

The rain is steady and strong again by the time we finish our supper, so we decide to try an Uber ride for the first time in our life. I open the app on my phone and follow what I think are the right steps to request a car. We walk to the front door to watch the rain and wait for our ride to arrive. I look down at the app and realize that it's telling me that our car has arrived. Looking outside, there waiting for us is a nice Prius with a young man inside beckoning us toward him.

Yep, turns out this is the car I just ordered through Uber. That fast. Six dollars later we're dropped off back at the Beall, the app taking care of all the money exchange. I almost did what I've always done in that situation, which would have been to get the phone number for a cab company, call them, wait for 20 minutes while they found a cab for me, taken the cab, hoped I had the right cash to pay him, and then arrived at my destination. But instead, we threw ourselves into this new technology called Uber, and by golly, it works.

Old dogs can, I suppose, learn new tricks.

EPILOGUE

It's a big day for Julie and Chris (my sister and her husband), as well as for their daughter Caysi, who's getting married today. Christine and I park on the side of the gravel road that ends at their farmhouse and stroll up the shaded drive. I wander into the house, which is buzzing with energy and activity, and say my hello to some of the folks I know, then exit the cramped kitchen out into the yard, where Christine waits for me away from the crowds.

I'm reminded of Julie's wedding to Chris about three decades ago, similarly held outdoors with a folksy and simple feel to it. I think simple weddings like this are the best. People are here because they're close friends or family. Vast fortunes aren't being spent, and nobody's here to be seen or to look good. Well, except maybe Julie and Caysi, and they both look stunning. Their glow warms us all for acres around.

We wander over to the barnyard, which Chris has meticulously transformed into a well-groomed little meadow for his daughter's nuptials. He's built a wedding canopy out of what appears to be hedge saplings and branches twisted together, and the pews consist of 2x10 planks laid across two-string bales of hay. Down the aisles are potted flowers, lovingly dug by the groom's mother from her garden along the walkway to their farmhouse up in Iowa.

It's a glorious Kansas afternoon, and I stroll around meeting new people. I've never met the groom, and many of the folks that I meet are family and friends of his. Some of the folks I meet are friends of the bride's, people I've either never met before, or whom I've met but have forgotten. It's always awkward trying to figure out one from the other as I make eye contact and approach someone, wondering if either of us remembers meeting the other in some past decade. Fortunately, many of the folks I meet are somewhere close to my age and consequently are familiar with the defects and shortcomings of memory that have forced us to keep more than 60 years' worth of stuff organized.

I meet a fella named George, an old family friend who has come out here from his home west of here in Kansas. He and I settle into a friendly conversation, learning a bit about each other, and it's not long before we're talking about the bike trip that Christine and I took across the Katy Trail a month ago.

George is familiar with the concept of building bike trails along old railroad right-of-ways, and our conversation helps to gel some of the thoughts that have been rattling around in my brain since our ride across the Katy. Those unorganized thoughts started on that first day of our ride, when I tried to understand why the city of Clinton, Missouri, wouldn't have wanted the trailhead right downtown by their merchants rather than a mile away outside of town.

As with all things, we each have a paintbrush and a palette of paints with which we paint the world around us as we travel through it. It's pretty easy to stand in front of the picture I've painted and wonder why the rest of the world can't see the plain simple truth in that picture. But my brush and my colors might just be different from the guy I'm talking to.

To me, the rail-trail concept has always been a brilliant idea. Take an abandoned right-of-way that was essentially given to the railroad 100 years ago or more and convert it to a biking path. The cost is dramatically reduced since a contiguous strip of land is owned, with railroad companies often willing to give it away (or at the very least sell it at a reasonable cost), and the grade has already been built. For towns along the path, it could be a great way to encourage some additional tourism through their town from time to time.

But from George's perspective, the idea of a rail trail is an invasion of what he believes to be his rights. George tells me that back where he lives, "a bunch of 'em" tried to build one of those trails through his area, but adds that "we're resisting as best we can." When I ask him to help me understand why the rail trail would be a bad idea, he lists two or three objections that are easily overcome with good design and good planning, but the real crux of his problem seems to come back to a real basic sense of "us" and "them," and a fear of change.

George has lived in his town for most of his life. It's his town, and anyone from the outside is, well, an outsider. It's okay that a county highway runs through town, because it's always been there, and mostly just local folks use it anyway. On the rare occasion when an outsider drives through, it's okay because they're just passing through. The idea that some folks who don't live in his town would build a bicycle trail that runs right through his town, bringing outsiders on bicycles through his world, represents an invasion of sorts to George. And then there's the land issue. Turns out his brother operates a farm outside of town, and that railroad right-of-way cuts right through his brother's farm. His brother is upset that the land that's part of the right-of-way didn't just get deeded over to him. While the railroad right-of-way was essentially public property that the railroad was given permission to use, and it existed long before George's brother owned that farm, I can see how he would still see it as "his" land.

I point out to George that folks who'd use the trail are just folks like me and Christine, for the most part. Hale and healthy folks, probably more safe on average than the general population. Does he really think that folks like me represent a threat? Not to mention that the cyclists who come through town are far more likely to actually spend money in town and help the local economy than are the folks who fly through in their car.

The picture I'm painting feels synergistic to me, like the world is full of commerce and opportunity and beauty and we should be able to share it all. But the picture George has is quite different. It's one where progress has eroded the world he's familiar with, and where outsiders too often represent more risk than opportunity. For him, the notion of a trail, and the people who come with it, is a threat. They're "them," and they threaten the "us" that George is familiar with. It reminds me of myself, and probably most folks, when we move into a nice area; as the years pass we get upset with all the new people who're coming in and building new homes and messing up this wonderful place we have. We establish a sense of *home*, and we don't want that home invaded by *others*.

I'm also reminded of Mitch back at the western trailhead in Clinton, who carried a gun out of fear of bad guys on the trail. The odds of running into some sort of bad guy out in the rural Midwest along a bicycle trail seemed pretty darned remote to me. Yet to Mitch, who'd ridden the trail for years, there was some underlying fear of some "other" whom he had to protect against.

How'd we get this way in America? What happened to the sense of country and community that I remember from when I was younger? How is it that folks who live in one of the safest regions in one of the safest countries in the world suddenly have such fear of others? How much does the pace of modern media play into the drastic difference that can exist in the way George and I see the notion of a rail trail?

When I was a child, television and radio existed, but they weren't a ubiquitous force in my life. Certainly no other forms of electronic media existed. We got your news primarily from the newspaper and while there were accepted biases on the editorial page, the papers worked hard to report the news objectively. Phones were attached to the wall, and many folks had a party line, meaning more than one household shared a single line (which led to some fun eavesdropping now and then.) We might sit down and watch a show one or two evenings a week, but most evenings (in good weather at least) were spent out in the shade on lawn chairs, chewing the fat with friends and neighbors. Neighbors might still develop color palettes that differed from one another slightly, and brushes might be slightly different, but folks tended to develop their perspectives in conversation with one another. A person could see the perspectives of the other person because everyone painted the pictures of the world in conversation with one another. Even if the pictures were different, they got painted during conversation, enjoying hospitality and friendship.

Today most of us paint our picture of the world around us based on some onslaught of media words and images. Hopefully most people try and validate information across several reliable sources before believing it, but all too often folks just choose their favorite source or two and believe whatever that source feeds them. The picture they have of the world around them is painted by the constant feed of information from the sources that tell them what they want to believe.

George finds his seat, and I find mine. The wedding is flawless, one of the most beautiful weddings I can remember. When it's over, folks make their way back to their cars and trucks, and four or five of us start hauling the planks and the bales of hay into the barn. I'm pretty sure that hay bales were lighter than this when I was younger, and with each bale I carry, I become more sure.

A couple of hours later, we're at the community center in north Topeka, where the reception is held. A simple affair, largely potluck. The toasts and the roasts are finished, supper completed, and the dancing has begun. Most of us are feeling pretty mellowed-out by the abundance of Budweiser. I feel a hand on my shoulder, and I turn to see George standing behind me.

"You look like you could use a beer," he says, pointing at my empty bottle. He hands me a fresh one and smiles.

I stand to chat with him, the crowd around us forcing us to be close enough to hear each other.

"Hey listen," he says when I'm done thanking him, "I wanted to tell you how much I appreciate the conversation we had earlier. I think maybe I'll take another look at that bike trail project when I get back home."

"Thanks George," I say with a smile, lifting my longneck up for a toast. "I really appreciated the conversation too. And you know what? I do think that trail users—especially those from the city—need to be educated on good common sense, manners, and ethics when it comes to respecting rural private property and small-town values."

He lifts his bottle and taps it against mine. "I guess old dogs can sometimes learn something new, huh?"

I nod. "Here's to old dogs."

George moves along to visit with someone else, and I sit back down. Serious redneck dancing is happening up on the dance floor, and well-lubricated conversation spills across every corner of the room. Children run free, sometimes on the dance floor, sometimes racing between tables. Parents are absolutely certain that inside these walls, only friends are present. This is community.

THE
END

ACKNOWLEDGMENTS

My name is on this book as its author, and I am completely responsible for the content. However, putting a book together takes a village. As an independent publisher I like to do as much as I can on my own in order to control costs. However, there are some things that I'll never be good at, and need the help of some very talented people to make it happen.

Erin Willard edits my work. Without her deft touch (which often feels endearingly ruthless) my work would be far less entertaining and readable than it is. Should the reader find any spot in this book that appears to have been missed by an editor, rest assured that Erin most likely suggested an edit, and the author chose to ignore the suggestion. Erin, please accept both my apologies and my thanks.

Ann Weinstock designed the cover for this book, as she has done for my previous cycling books. I am lucky to have her as a partner, as she brings my covers to light in ways that I could never imagine on my own.

Kim Horgan is a cyclist who lives in the Kansas City area, as well as a phenomenal photographer. She is the creator of several of the images used in this book, as well as the beautiful cover image of the bicycle on the bridge. These images are used with her kind permission.

A tale of journey is made good mostly by the people who appear along the path. As such, this book is made better by the many people who helped it become a story. Thanks to Kathy at the Main Street Inn, Mitch along the trail, Roger and Annette at the Haysler House in Clinton, Kriss and Gene at the High Street Victorian House Bed & Breakfast in Boonville, George and his guests at the Palace restaurant in Boonville, James in Rocheport, Leaia and Mark at the Globe Hotel in Hartsburg, Liz at the Cliff Manor Inn in Jeff City, the shopkeeper in Mokane, Christine Cady at the Cady Winterset Cottage, the staff at the Hermann Wurst Haus along with the folks at Simon's On the Waterfront. Thanks also to the great folks at Philly's Pizza in Marthasville, Chuck and Esther at the Red Brick Inn in Augusta along with all the great folks in Augusta who made Rick and I feel wonderful at their annual bash. Thanks to Jodi and Tony at the Bike Stop Café in St Charles and to Jim and Sandy Belote at the Beall Mansion in Alton.

Somehow stories that involve my brother seem to crop up in every book I write. I suppose that has to do with all the fun adventures I've had with him over the years, or maybe it has to do with how much he means to me. Either way, my deep thanks to Erik for letting me share so many stories of our adventures and misadventures, and to his wife Ellen for appearing in this adventure.

Thanks to Rick Becker for his life-long friendship, and for letting me tell so much about us and to make a little fun of us in this book as I wax on about one of those rare occasions when we get to spend a little time together. Thanks for sharing portions of the ride with me Rick.

My dear wife Christine provides a first level of feedback and criticism, for which I am extremely grateful. Most importantly, thank you Christine for your companionship in sharing the joy of the ride upon which this book is based. Your willingness and enthusiasm for each new adventure is a delight in my life.

WHAT DID YOU THINK?

Indie authors rely almost exclusively on word-of-mouth referrals to grow our audience. Your feedback in the form of a review on Amazon or Goodreads will be greatly appreciated. In addition, I'd love your feedback directly: NeilHansonAuthor@gmail.com

Buy Pilgrim Wheels - The first part of the journey story based on my cross country trip, from Monterey on the west coast to Medicine Lodge in Kansas.

Buy Pilgrim Spokes - The conclusion of the journey story based on my cross country trip, from Medicine Lodge in Kansas to Annapolis on the east coast.

Buy The Pilgrim Way - The nuts and bolts essential guide to minimalist bicycle touring. Includes turn by turn directions for the route that Neil took across America.

Thank you for supporting Neil M Hanson as an independent author, and for supporting High Prairie Press as a small indie publisher committed to bringing voices to the marketplace who speak through The Art of Truth. Your reviews at Amazon and elsewhere are greatly appreciated!

ABOUT THE AUTHOR

Author and speaker Neil Hanson is a lifelong cyclist. His two-wheeled adventures have taken him across America, along the Natchez Trace, across several of the nations premier rail trails, and throughout northern Italy.

The Flint Hills of Kansas are home to Neil. The wide rolling landscape of the deep tallgrass prairie taught him to cultivate a broad perspective while searching for subtleties hidden in low pockets sheltered from the winds of what feels obvious.

He graduated from Kansas State University, where he studied Architecture and Psychology. A short stint with an engineering firm taught him that sitting in one place and doing one thing probably wasn't going to work for him, so he began a meandering career path to which he's remained true. He's worked as a cook, carpenter, truck driver, concrete finisher, salesman, operations manager, computer programmer, and project manager. His executive experience included several years in c-level positions. He currently works as a project manager for one of the finest and largest providers of healthcare in the country.

Neil lives in Colorado, where he navigates his bicycle up and down the inclines of the Rocky Mountains. He writes early in the morning, rides his bike as often as he can, hunts and fishes a bit, and spins yarns at every opportunity.

Upcoming projects include cycling books about the Natchez

Trace in Mississippi, Alabama, and Tennessee, and the Mickelson Trail in South Dakota. Recently he and his wife Christine have taken up sailing as their newest exploit, and spend as much time as they can on the Eastern Shore of the Chesapeake with their newfound adventure. He's looking forward to helping these new escapades find their way across his keyboard and onto the pages of books and articles in coming years.

BOOKS BY NEIL HANSON

Most of what Neil writes falls into the Creative Nonfiction category, just like this one. He likes to call it the Art of Truth. It's reflective storytelling; searching for insight, wrestling with experience for wisdom and perspective.

THE CYCLING REFLECTIONS SERIES

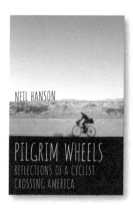

Pilgrim Wheels (2015) — Book one in the series is a deep exploration of the western half of Neil's bicycle journey across America, beginning in Monterey, California, and concluding in Medicine Lodge, Kansas. This is a book for those who enjoy thoughtful stories focused on the experience of the journey more than the details of the ride. (For the "how-to" description of the bicycle ride, see The Pilgrim Way, below.)
https://www.amazon.com/dp/B00SXIK-9WK

Pilgrim Spokes (2016) — Book two is a deep exploration of the eastern half of Neil's bicycle journey across America, beginning in Medicine Lodge, Kansas, and concluding in Annapolis, Maryland. This is a journey story like Pilgrim Wheels, though this one is also a deeply personal tale of transition.
https://www.amazon.com/dp/B01DW-PRW5U

Cycling Across America: The Pilgrim Bundle (2018) The complete Pilgrim Boxed Set including both Pilgrim Wheels and Pilgrim Spokes, as well as a new preface. Available electronically initially.

https://www.amazon.com/Cycling-Across-America-Books-Reflections-ebook/dp/B07B65VP3Q/

THE WANDERING WHEELIST SERIES

The Pilgrim Way (2015) — A turn-by-turn description of the logistics, route, and details of Neil's journey across America. It's an essential guide for those considering long-distance bicycle touring in general or a cross-country trek specifically. Images taken during the journey are included in the print edition.

https://www.amazon.com/dp/ B00SP5W-M7Q

Cycling the Katy Trail (2018) — This hybrid is a new kind of cycling book, combining a trail guide in the first half of the book with a journey story in the second half of the book. Join Neil and his wife Christine as they explore the Katy Trail in Missouri from one end to the other, delighting in this jewel of the American rail-trail system.

Cycling the Natchez Trace (Planned for 2019) — Neil and Dave continue their sojourning, this time on the Natchez Trace and joined by Neil's son Ian. From Baton Rouge to Nashville, Neil explores what can only be described as a national treasure for the cyclist.

NON-CYCLING BOOKS

Peace at the Edge of Uncertainty (2010) — Neil's first book is a spiritual story of transition woven around the final days and hours that he shares with his dying father and the mystical events that are part of that experience.

https://www.amazon.com/dp/B003N3V01E